When Law and Religion Meet

The Point of Convergence

April L. Bogle and Ginger Pyron

Center *for the* Study *of* Law *and* Religion
at Emory University

The Center for the Study of Law and Religion brings together scholars and students, policy-makers and the public to explore the interaction of law and religion.

This convergence builds new bridges of dialogue among the finest existing and emerging minds, establishes new libraries of knowledge and forums of public discussion, and generates objective information and reasoned opinions on contentious public policy issues.

Religion gives law its spirit and inspires its adherence to ritual, tradition, and justice.

Law gives religion its structure and encourages its devotion to order, organization, and orthodoxy.

Law and religion share such ideas as fault, obligation, and covenant and such methods as ethics, rhetoric, and textual interpretation.

Law and religion balance each other by counterpoising justice and mercy, rule and equity, discipline and love.

For Harold J. Berman,

our Chief

Published 2007 by

Wm. B. Eerdmans Publishing Co.

2140 Oak Industrial Drive N.E., Grand Rapids, Michigan 49505 /

P.O. Box 163, Cambridge CB3 9PU U.K.

Printed in the United States of America

12 11 10 09 08 07 7 6 5 4 3 2 1

ISBN 978-0-8028-6294-5

www.eerdmans.com

Table of Contents

A student in law school went to a law professor and asked, "In the midst of all these rules and regulations, where will I find discussions of justice?" The professor answered, "If you want justice, go to divinity school."

The student went to divinity school and took courses—New Testament, the Acts of Jesus, Patristic and Systematic Theology—then asked a theology professor, "In the midst of all this, where will I find discussions of justice?" The professor replied, "If it's justice you're after, go to law school."

Frank S. Alexander, *Founding Director*
Center for the Study of Law and Religion
Emory University

IN THE BEGINNING

Law. Religion. Oh, yes, they knew of each other, these two old dignitaries. But until the 1970s their intercourse consisted of a stiff nod in passing, at best. Like divergent and somewhat disdainful cultures, they chose not to mingle.

A prescient few, though, realized that these two crusty autocrats might benefit from dialogue and, furthermore, that the separate spheres of law and religion would soon overlap in unprecedented ways.

Gifted with resources, opportunity, and sufficient cheek, these few invited law and religion to the same table—and started asking questions that even isolationists couldn't ignore.

THE GENESIS

The Visionary

"My deep conviction—in fact, my passion—was that the university should be a scene of fertile intellectual conversation, where different disciplines fortify each other's imagination and thought," said **James T. "Jim" Laney**, president emeritus of Emory University. "The University of Chicago had initiated a cross-disciplinary approach, resulting in a climate of intellectual ferment. I wanted to re-create that at Emory.

Jim Laney (left) with Robert W. Woodruff, 1978

"The university, I think, also has a moral calling to work toward the larger good. That role includes unmasking the hidden assumptions and accepted wisdom from the past, to help us better understand what's going on in the present. From there, our responsibility is to educate the public and thus to inform decision making.

"My role as president was to plant a seed for such work and to provide some resources, which arrived with an infusion of capital funds from the Woodruff gift. Since there were no restrictions on that gift, we were able to be innovative. And one of the innovations I was most interested in was the conversation between law and religion."

The Catalyst

In the mid-1970s **Frank S. Alexander**, a recent graduate of the University of North Carolina at Chapel Hill, was working on civil rights issues in Atlanta. He already knew Laney, then dean of Candler School of Theology at Emory, because while still at UNC Alexander had written to Laney "sight unseen," asking the dean to act as advisor for his senior thesis. While in Atlanta, he sought Laney's advice again: "I've been accepted to Harvard's Law School and Divinity School. Which field should I study?" Laney's succinct reply: "Both." Despite Harvard's lack of a structured joint degree program in law and theology, Alexander complied. As he worked on both a law degree and a master of theological studies, he found a mentor in Harvard Law professor Harold J. "Hal" Berman—one of the few legal scholars in the United States at that time willing to write about law and religion.

The Magnet

Harold J. Berman, a long-established authority on Soviet law and international trade, held several other distinctions among Harvard's law faculty. Brought up as a Jew, he became a Christian after experiencing a life-changing vision of Christ. At a time when law and religion together was a taboo subject in law schools, he insisted on the significant mutual influence of the two fields, initiating the seminal scholarship on their interaction. And in the early 1980s, as he neared retirement age, he resisted Harvard's rule that at age 65, professors received emeritus status but had to leave the classroom: "Rather than be put on the shelf and ignored, I was determined to keep teaching. I knew that I still had many books to add to the shelf." Berman was right about that, having published 10 books and more than 100 articles since coming to Emory. What he didn't know, as he responded kindly to a letter from a student at Calvin College, was how closely someone else's future was linked with his.

The Standard-Bearer

An undergraduate approaching graduation at Calvin College in 1982, **John Witte, Jr.,** had read and admired the work of Hal Berman on law and religion. Out of the blue, he wrote Berman a long letter explaining his interests and aspirations and asking whether, as his next step, he should attend law school at Yale or Harvard, or pursue graduate work in philosophy. In three days, Berman sent Witte a two-page handwritten reply, counseling him to come to Harvard and offering him a research assistantship: "There I was, just some 21-year-old punk, and this great man took the time to write to me, even giving me the grace of an invitation to work with him." Witte gladly took the advice, the assistantship, the gift of grace, and the fork in the road that would definitively shape not only his own life, but an entire field of scholarship.

I wish you every success in your spiritual and intellectual pilgrimage into the world of law. ... most of all, my young friend, keep your faith and find a place for it in your legal learning, for only then will you find rest for your reason and for your conscience.

Excerpt from **Harold J. Berman's** letter to undergraduate **John Witte, Jr.,** February 1982

THE CONVERGENCE

After completing his degrees in law and theology at Harvard, Alexander came to Atlanta again—this time to stay. "Five years after having finished both law school and divinity school, I was teaching as an adjunct professor in law and theology, and practicing law here in Atlanta. Along the way I'd had discussions with Emory administrators about the possibility of creating a joint degree program." One day in the summer of 1982, Alexander stopped by to visit with Laney, who had become Emory's president. Laney said, "Isn't it time for us to start a law and religion program here at Emory?" Alexander agreed.

Frank's interests intersected in many ways with mine—a passion for religion, for commitment, for values, for meaning in life. And he had such a marvelous sense of the discipline of law itself, both its practice and its potential—not just as a vehicle to be exploited for aggrandizement but as a promotion of the larger public good. He was determined to see that law worked for the good of society.

Jim Laney

Frank Alexander with students, 1987

As was typical of his leadership style, Laney scouted for the very best talent to help lead this new program. He found it in Harold Berman, one of the country's ranking law professors. Berman's radical series of lectures at Boston University, published in 1974 as *The Interaction of Law and Religion*, had laid the foundation for the program Laney and Alexander longed to create. In 1985, Berman received not one, but two nominations—from the department of Soviet Studies and from the Law School—for Emory's first Robert W. Woodruff Professorship. Laney made the offer. Berman accepted. Suddenly the young Law and Religion Program acquired national status. "Jim Laney made it clear that I could stay at Harvard and rest on my laurels, or I could go to Emory and help build something new. I knew immediately what I wanted," said Berman.

Hal Berman at a reception welcoming him to Emory, 1984

> *Hal Berman brought a great historical perspective, establishing our program's legitimacy within the legal order and among the faculty. He was able to interpret the interaction of law and religion in a way that won enormous support across the university, across the nation, and throughout the world.*
>
> Jim Laney

"I came to Emory in 1985 as a stowaway in Hal Berman's briefcase," said Witte about his arrival in Atlanta. Even with his new law degree from Harvard and a growing list of scholarly publications, Witte was still something of a dark horse in the field of law and religion, and he knew it. After serving as a research fellow in legal history for a year, he entered legal practice. Nine months later came the windfall: "President Laney called and said, 'We have the unique opportunity to make religion a legitimate part of serious discourse in any profession, any discipline, any department on the Emory campus. I would like you to help lead the discussion of religion in the law school. We have path-breakers already in place: Frank Alexander has created the Law and Religion Program; Hal Berman is here to work with you as well. I want you to direct this program, to build it up in concert with them.' I was still a youngster and recognized my inadequacies. But I thought, here's a crack in the door, a chance for me to prove myself. Teaching. Scholarship. Advancing new areas of research. Dazzled, I didn't hear what the salary was. I didn't hear what the responsibilities were. I just said 'yes.' "

One of John's gifts as director is to set the standards very high. But he never asks of others what he isn't willing to do 10 times over himself. He expects us to come together, learn from each other, then do more than we have ever done before in communicating our research and understanding to others. The quality of work that arises from these standards is what makes people throughout the world eager to be a part of this Center.

Frank Alexander

John Witte (left) with Frank Alexander, 1993

From Laney's vision and discerning choices, something unique had arisen at Emory—a rich and groundbreaking interdisciplinary exchange, anchored in three uncannily well-matched leaders: Alexander, with his ardent mission of combining law and social activism into a law-based ministry; Berman, with his trailblazing, panoramic scholarship on the Western legal tradition and its underlying belief-systems; and Witte, with what Laney calls "his laser-like mind, sweeping historical and legal perspective, galvanizing vision, and soaring standards for scholarship, teaching, and collegiality."

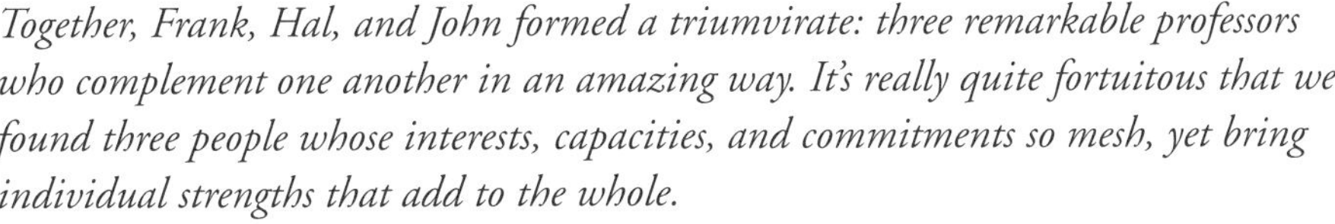

Together, Frank, Hal, and John formed a triumvirate: three remarkable professors who complement one another in an amazing way. It's really quite fortuitous that we found three people whose interests, capacities, and commitments so mesh, yet bring individual strengths that add to the whole.

Jim Laney

All four of these innovators shared a zeal to prove wrong the pervasive assumption in the academy that God was dead, that religion had become irrelevant, and that the future belonged to reason and science. They wanted to show, instead, that the work and spirit of religion had *everything* to do with the work and spirit of law; that the two, in fact, were inseparably linked.

As the crescent enterprise tackled its first questions—*where do we set up our space? what funding should we seek? which projects will entice and engage scholars from other disciplines? what forums will propel our work into academic and public awareness?*—these old strangers, Law and Religion, began to share a conversation, an office, and a destiny.

Two far-seeing mentors. Their protégés, two rising stars. At Emory, the cosmic tumblers clicked into place.

Director

John Witte, Jr.

J.D., Harvard University

Jonas Robitscher Professor of Law and Ethics, Emory University

In directing a research project, I like to let each participant play to his or her specialty, and open their scholarly world for us. Then I push them to think beyond their traditional categories of knowledge in writing something fresh, and then build a responsible architecture that holds together these multiple-specialty contributions to the project.

Beyond his gifts as an administrator, Witte is an acclaimed specialist in legal history, marriage law, religious liberty, religion and human rights, and Christian jurisprudence. He has published 120 articles and 20 books so far—not counting their translations into eight languages. Skyrocketing the Center's reputation, he has lectured and convened conferences throughout North America, Europe, Israel, Japan, and South Africa, and has won numerous major awards for his research. In the classroom, too, he's a star: The Emory Law School students have voted him the year's Most Outstanding Professor nine times, and he also has received Emory University's Emory Williams Award, Crystal Apple Award, and University Scholar and Teacher Award.

Witte's colleagues at the Center describe him as an anchor, a driver, an entrepreneur, a formidable administrator, an excellent scholar, a catalyst of people's scholarship. Center Senior Fellow Abdullahi An-Na'im says, "Every time I come to John with an idea, I leave with an idea that's much larger and better. He has the knack of asking the right questions. He quickly grasps the idea, engages with it, and then he probes some more—turning it around into something much finer."

"One of the great things John Witte has done," adds University of Chicago scholar and Center visiting professor Don Browning, "is insisting that to get this conversation going—to bring law more to the attention of practical religion, and religion more to the attention of law—you've got to dig into the history."

One of the finest tributes to Witte comes from Hal Berman, who in a 2007 memo to the Emory Law faculty, thanking them for celebrating his 60th year as a law school teacher, wrote these words: "The best thing I ever did as a law school teacher was to reply to a college senior, who in early 1982, wrote a long letter to me. ... May you all be blessed with research assistants—and eventually colleagues—like John Witte!"

John Witte, Jr.

"We are not here to proselytize our faith. We are not introducing a soft subject that dilutes or distracts from rigorous legal study. We are not trying to create room for given fundamentalist agendas. Instead, we genuinely seek to sponsor a deeper and richer understanding of law, by increasing understanding of the fundamental role religion has played in shaping law, politics, and society."

Founding Director
Frank S. Alexander
J.D./M.T.S., Harvard University
Professor of Law, Emory University

The work of law and religion allows me to understand my ministry and to interpret it; but my work as a practicing attorney—which I view as a ministry—also informs my understanding of law and faith. I can't do one without the other.

In 1982, Alexander founded Emory's internationally renowned Law and Religion Program, a weighty achievement he describes with characteristic self-effacement: "I was a doorstop. My role was to prop open the door for students and faculty to begin the inquiry into the interaction of law and religion." His influence, however, reaches far and wide.

Besides opening doors for countless scholars and students throughout the world, Alexander is one of the nation's leading scholars on homelessness and housing, focusing on affordable housing, urban redevelopment, and state and local government law. He has published numerous articles in his areas of specialty and has received more than 20 awards for his teaching and public service, including the University's Emory Williams Award, Crystal Apple Award, and the University Scholar and Teacher Award. With an unflagging commitment to his personal ministry that combines faith, social justice, and legal counsel, Alexander also served as a fellow of the Carter Center of Emory University from 1993-1996, and as a Commissioner of the State Housing Trust Fund for the Homeless from 1994-1998. (See related text, page 53.)

"For me, where law and religion lead is the call to respond in service to those who are facing really tough issues, and to do so with all of the resources of legal and religious traditions."

Frank S. Alexander

Harold J. Berman
J.D., Yale University
Robert W. Woodruff Professor of Law, Emory University
CSLR Senior Fellow

If we want to give a legal foundation to this new world economy and this new world society—which someday will become, I hope, a world community—we've got to go back to human nature and the spiritual values we hold in common.

Sage, father, "Chief": In such reverend terms, professors acknowledge Berman's decades of pioneering work in the field of law and religion. Berman came to Emory in 1985 from Harvard, where he taught for 37 years and is now James Barr Ames Professor of Law Emeritus. At a time when religion was dismissed as irrelevant to legal study, he broached the relationship between law and religion not only with courage and depth but with a foresight that time has vindicated.

Central to Berman's lifetime of work is the idea of belief—whether or not it includes traditional religious faith. He tells this story: "Not long ago I was speaking in China, where law schools are pouring forth lawyers in the hundreds of thousands. They asked me to speak about the Western tradition, about law and religion. During the discussion period after my speech, a scholar stood up and asked, 'In order to have a legal tradition, do we have to believe in God?' I said, 'No, but you have to believe in something. You have to believe in law.'"

A believer by several definitions, Berman himself passionately believes in the power of law to help correct global societal inequities and to establish systems of trust, peace, and cooperation. He has produced more than 300 articles and 24 books, including the prize-winning *Law and Revolution: The Formation of the Western Legal Tradition* (1983) and its sequel, *Law and Revolution II: The Impact of the Protestant Reformation on the Western Legal Tradition* (2003). He's a fellow of the Carter Center of Emory University, with a special focus in U.S.-Russian relations. He also directs the World Law Institute of Emory University, which conducts research and sponsors programs in world law; and is founder and director of the American Law Center in Moscow, which offers instruction in American law for Russian lawyers. As a leading authority on comparative legal history, jurisprudence, Russian law, and international trade law—and as a scholar whom Jim Laney calls "one of the great polymaths of American legal education"—Berman has lectured widely in the United States, Europe, and Asia, and his writings have appeared in more than 20 languages.

In the past 60 years, Berman, who refers to teaching as his "calling," has taught more than 10,000 students. More than 250 of them are now teaching in law schools around the world. Senior Fellow Michael J. Broyde captures the awe that marks many professors' and students' response to this venerable scholar: "In 1946, Hal

Berman, while still a student at Yale Law School, wrote for the *Yale Law Journal* an article on the law of marriage and divorce in Soviet Russia. Fifty-five years later, I found myself here at Emory, writing a Jewish gloss on that piece. I could never have imagined that I would have the honor of becoming his colleague."

Harold J. Berman

"My own interest now is, above all, in the coming together of the different cultures of the world. We have to find common spiritual values to hold us together or we may destroy each other with our nuclear weapons."

James T. Laney
Ph.D., M.Div., Yale University
President Emeritus, Emory University

In the last few decades we've learned that the "rational man" is a conceit that needs to be discarded. How to deal with that shift imaginatively and creatively and successfully is something we continue to explore.

With this same series of adverbs, Laney might have summed up his own handling of all life's sticklers. According to Laney's biographer, "Time and again in interviews, those who worked closely with Laney ... marvel at his capacity to convey a vision. They describe him as being tough-minded, imaginative, creative, and persuasive in the conveying of that message." (F. Stuart Gulley, *The Academic President as Moral Leader: James T. Laney at Emory University, 1977-1993*). In fact, Gulley continues, "An outstanding characteristic of Laney's presidency was his ability to articulate a vision and gain the support of others." This gift has graced Laney's entire and highly influential life.

His pre-Emory years included teaching at Yonsei University in Seoul as a Methodist missionary, earning a Ph.D. in Christian Ethics at Yale, and teaching at the Divinity School of Vanderbilt University. Emory first welcomed Laney as dean of Candler School of Theology. During his 16 years as Emory's president, Laney sought the support of others—time and again, indeed—to create a richer intellectual climate through collaboration among the disciplines, and to help the university become a moral community concerned with advancing the common good. Both of those goals met with remarkable success in the founding of the Law and Religion Program.

Later, having guided Emory's maturation into a top-tier research university with an endowment that had multiplied tenfold, Laney returned to Korea as a U.S. Ambassador under President Bill Clinton, where he was instrumental in helping resolve the nuclear crisis with North Korea in 1994. Receiving the Department of Defense Distinguished Service Medal in 1997, he was praised by Secretary of Defense William J. Perry for—not surprisingly—his "unprecedented leadership and visionary guidance during a time of crisis."

Laney is an ordained United Methodist minister and continues his life's work as visionary, motivator, and moral leader. He co-chaired the Council on Foreign Relations Task Force on Korea, chaired the Board of Overseers Committee for the Divinity School at Harvard, and served on the University Council at Yale. He currently is a trustee of the Henry Luce Foundation and the Carter Center of Emory University.

James T. Laney

"I think the role of the university is not only to analyze but also in some instances to unmask the hidden assumptions and accepted wisdom of the past."

EARLY ALLIES AND ADVISORS

In its early years, the Law and Religion Program owed much to the support of two instrumental people at Emory:

Howard O. "Woody" Hunter
J.D., Yale University
Dean, Emory University School of Law, 1989-2001
Interim Provost and Executive Vice President for Academic Affairs, Emory University, 2001-2003

"A gentle and generous soul behind the scenes," in Witte's words, and the well-loved and highly accomplished dean of Emory Law School, Hunter shared Laney's commitment to interdisciplinary thought. He staunchly supported and protected the law and religion alliance across campus and promoted the interaction of law and economics, psychology, politics, and literature. And he brought to Emory a number of the key law faculty who led the expansion of the Law and Religion Program, including Abdullahi An-Na'im, Michael J. Broyde, and Johan D. van der Vyver.

Because he saw law and religion as an important part of a holistic legal education, he helped find funding for the young program, steadily moving it forward. "Without Woody," Witte says, "the program never would have come into its own." Hunter is now the president of Singapore Management University.

Rebecca S. Chopp
Ph.D., University of Chicago
Dean of Faculty and Academic Affairs,
Candler School of Theology, 1993-1997
Provost and Executive Vice President for Academic Affairs,
Emory University, 1998-2002

"Rebecca had an unusual appetite for the counter-intuitive, mold-breaking approach to a topic. A good example was her leadership in building feminist theology, at a time when that field was unfashionable," said Witte. That propensity made her a valuable early ally of the emerging program in law and religion—first as an interested faculty participant, then as a supportive academic dean of the theology school, and most influentially as Emory's provost.

Witte considers Chopp the major force behind the expansion of the Law and Religion Program. "She took the step of working with us to secure funding from The Pew

Charitable Trusts, so that we could make the Law and Religion Program a Center, add the professional staff members who have been so vital to its success, and support our first big new international projects on 'Sex, Marriage, and Family' and 'The Child in Law, Religion, and Society.'" Since 2002, Chopp has served as the president of Colgate University.

Longstanding Emory professors, now senior fellows of the Center for the Study of Law and Religion, these scholars offered both early and ongoing encouragement to the Law and Religion Program, contributing generously of their expertise, wisdom, and heartening presence:

David R. Blumenthal
Ph.D., Columbia University
Jay and Leslie Cohen Professor of Judaic Studies, Emory University
CSLR Senior Fellow

Blumenthal, a dynamic interdisciplinary leader on campus, has also served as a valuable "town-gown" bridge, particularly within the Jewish community. He's a straightforward counselor and a sage critic, with an extraordinary ability to create a common table for people of historically divided factions and to draw them into open, honest, and learned discussion. He teaches and writes on constructive Jewish theology, medieval Judaism, Jewish mysticism, and Holocaust studies.

Jon P. Gunnemann
Ph.D., Yale University
Professor of Social Ethics, Emory University
CSLR Senior Fellow

A natural teacher and a wise and winsome counselor, Gunnemann pursues a broad interest in professional ethics, including the intersection of law, theology, business, and medicine—their shared questioning, their similar ethical issues, and their common need to develop a methodology of ethical reflection and implementation. Currently, he's researching theology, ethics, and the economy, as well as contemporary theories of justice. Gunnemann has written extensively on issues of business ethics and social theory.

M. Thomas Thangaraj
Th.D., Harvard Divinity School
D.W. and Ruth Brooks Professor of World Christianity
Emory University
CSLR Senior Fellow

From his early experiences as a Christian missionary child in India, Thangaraj knows firsthand what it's like to live as a Christian minority in both a Hindu and an Islamic culture. Deeply receptive to multiple ways of expressing common religious sentiments, he has made a career of interpreting the Hindu world for Christians and the Christian world for Hindus, helping to widen the program's intellectual, geographic, and confessional scope. His current research includes an ethnographic study of inculturation of the gospel in South India, and the development of a systematic theology from a cross-cultural perspective.

Steven M. Tipton
Ph.D., Harvard University
Professor of Sociology of Religion, Emory University
Director of the Graduate Division of Religion
CSLR Senior Fellow

Gifted with an encyclopedic mind and an astonishing memory, Tipton can associate ideas that most people wouldn't consider together, then interweave them into a tapestry of extraordinary new learning. He brims with both ideas and context, currently applying his gymnastic intellect to research on the institutional logics of American religion and politics, and on the sociology of morality. Tipton helped lead the Center's two most recent projects, on marriage, family, and children.

Well conceived, well staffed, well supported. With leaders well convinced that their program could open thinking worldwide.

They were ready to prove it.

THE BURDEN OF PROOF

To the founders of the Law and Religion Program, the need for focused scholarship and teaching in this vital field of inquiry was paramount:

Where else could students and scholars learn the fundamentals of church and state, religion and politics, faith and order?

How could they learn to balance justice and mercy, rule and equity, discipline and love, in their work as legal and religious professionals?

Where could they come to understand the inner workings of Jewish, Christian, and Islamic laws, and their respective places in the modern nation-state and global order?

How could they explore the essential religious foundations and dimensions of law, politics, and society, in the West and beyond?

"We based the joint degree program in the legal academy, to boost legal education's receptivity to the idea of linking religion and law," recalls Alexander. "At that time virtually no law school in the country was doing serious scholarship or teaching related to religion. Indeed, most law schools were hostile to the study of theology, religion, and issues of church and state."

Witte adds: "There's a burden of proof against any new area of interdisciplinary discourse, especially in a law school. Interdisciplinary legal study needs to enhance the study of law, to open up new understanding of how law works in context and in concert with other disciplines. In the face of healthy suspicion, that's exactly how we had to portray the Law and Religion Program and to shape its projects.

"We are not proselytizing our faith. We are not introducing a soft subject that dilutes or distracts from rigorous legal study. We are not trying to create room for given fundamentalist agendas. Instead, we genuinely seek to sponsor a deeper and richer understanding of law, by increasing understanding of the fundamental role religion has played in shaping law, politics, and society."

Intent on asserting its legitimacy in academe and beyond, the established Law and Religion Program—eventually called the Center for the Study of Law and Religion (CSLR)—began a prodigious push toward productivity. Its proving grounds spanned interdisciplinary research projects, international conferences, and a fast-growing list of new scholarly books.

It was thought to be a tenet of the Modern Age: Sooner or later, religion would be consigned to the ash heap of history in favor of something a little more ... rational. [T]he very subject was seen as a curious, almost laughable relic of the past. ... Those prejudices, however, turned out to be childishly short-sighted. Not only did the intense flame of religious impulse fail to burn out. In many parts of the world, it has been fanned into a conflagration. ... Any lingering doubts about the need to study religion seriously went up in the flames erupting from the World Trade Center.

Trust magazine
The Pew Charitable Trusts
Winter 2004

Unflagging support has come from Emory University, particularly the Law School, the Theology School, the College, and the Office of the Provost. Extremely generous external support has flowed also from The Pew Charitable Trusts, the Ford Foundation, the Lilly Endowment, the Alonzo L. McDonald Family Foundation, the John Templeton Foundation, the Luce Foundation, and many other individual and institutional benefactors.

In 2000, The Pew Charitable Trusts awarded Emory a $3.2 million grant to establish the Center for the Study of Law and Religion (initially called the Center for the Interdisciplinary Study of Religion) as one of its 10 new Centers of Excellence in religious scholarship.

The Winter 2004 issue of Pew's *Trust* magazine explained that each Center of Excellence "examines religion through a slightly different thematic lens. And their influence goes beyond the walls of the academy, since they have a civic component that reaches out to policy-makers, journalists, and the public. All, in fact, contribute to what might be called a scholarly religious revival—which is not necessarily tied to personal religious convictions."

Through its teaching, research, and public education, the well-established, well-proven CSLR now comprises

- four joint degree programs (J.D./M.Div., J.D./M.T.S., J.D./M.A., and J.D./Ph.D.)
- 14 cross-listed courses
- eight major research projects; dozens of individual and side research projects
- six to nine annual public forums
- two book series
- 300-plus published volumes
- visiting scholars and fellows program
- 80 Emory senior fellows and associated faculty from 20 fields of study

MAJOR MULTI-YEAR RESEARCH PROJECTS

Affordable Housing and Community Development

Christian Legal Studies

Islamic Legal Studies

Jewish Legal Studies

Moral and Religious Foundations of Law

Religion and Human Rights

Sex, Marriage, and Family & the Religions of the Book

The Child in Law, Religion, and Society

For a full listing of all research projects and their participants, visit www.law.emory.edu/cslr.

Year after year, the Center's fresh approach, scholarly productivity, and increasing momentum have attracted generous affirmation and benefaction.

THE FOCUS

faith, freedom, and family –

the centerpieces of our lives,

the three things that people will fight for, die for

THE METHODS

retrieve the religious sources and dimensions of law, politics, and society in the Western tradition and beyond

reconstruct the most enduring teachings of the traditions for our day

re-engage a historically informed religious viewpoint with the hard issues that now confront church, state, and society

THE WORK

inter-religious in inspiration, with emphasis on the traditions of Judaism, Christianity, and Islam

interdisciplinary in perspective, seeking to bring the wisdom of religious traditions into greater conversation with law, public policy, and the humane and social sciences

international in orientation, seeking to situate American debates over interdisciplinary legal and religious issues within an emerging global conversation

AN OPEN FORUM

From its beginnings, the Law and Religion Program flung wide the doors of participation. Neither a pulpit nor a soapbox, it delivered no sermons, no sales pitches. Every flavor of Judaism, Christianity, and Islam, and every scholarly perspective were welcome at the table and lectern, so long as scientific rigor and open-minded candor prevailed. Viewed under a multidisciplinary lens, no ideological position was "safe," because at the Law and Religion Center the inherited assumptions of custom, culture, and tradition alike were liable to be challenged, even toppled, by new questions.

There's a **hadith**, a saying of the Prophet, that says it's a blessing of God that there is diversity among the opinions of one community. The modern translation says the disagreements among the scholars of my community are a blessing. So there is a strong tradition of Muslims celebrating the possibility of difference of opinion.

Abdullahi An-Na'im
Charles Howard Candler
Professor of Law,
Emory University
CSLR Senior Fellow

In the work of the Center for the Study of Law and Religion, that heady dynamic continues today. So far, more than 1,600 scholars worldwide have shared in CSLR conferences and research projects, and thousands more have directly encountered the Center's work either in reading books by CSLR professors or in attending lectures, conferences, and other public events. The Center's library shelves are bowing with scores of new thought-provoking volumes authored by senior fellows and project participants. Generous funding flows in. Around the common table, and in increasing numbers, people of reason and conscience open even wider the field, the forum, and the future.

As world events have made clear, law and religion are universal solvents of human living. Together they create a volatile compound, and sometimes when they come together in explosive ways, the world is imperiled. Studying this still-new branch of societal chemistry, the Center seeks ways to avert the danger without losing either the energy or the light.

Toward that end, the tasks are clear:

To liven the discourse;

To tackle tough questions of law, politics, and society;

To provide resources for better understanding across cultural and political chasms;

To help Jews, Christians, and Muslims—the three children of Abraham—recognize and reach each other through the fundamental questions shared by all.

POWERFUL VIEWPOINTS

This rapid expansion of the ambition and achievements in law and religion would not have been possible without the visionary leadership and remarkable energy of six new colleagues in law and religion who have joined the Emory community.

Abdullahi Ahmed An-Na'im
Ph.D., University of Edinburgh
L.L.B., University of Cambridge
L.L.B., University of Khartoum
Charles Howard Candler Professor of Law, Emory University
CSLR Senior Fellow

One of the most powerful entry points to a discourse about human rights in Islamic society is to invoke the Qur'annic imperative for social justice and say: Here is a pragmatic, sustainable way to achieve it in the modern context.

Abdullahi An-Na'im was a young law student in his home country of Sudan when he reached a personal deadlock over issues surrounding Islam. "I am a Muslim, but I couldn't accept Islamic law. I couldn't see how Sudan could be viable without women being full citizens and without non-Muslims being full citizens. ... I couldn't live with this view of Islam," he said in *The New Yorker* (September 11, 2006). The conflict led to his exile from Sudan.

A tireless activist as well as a courageous and esteemed scholar of international human rights, comparative constitutional law, and Islamic law, An-Na'im has spent the last 20 years working, often at a grass-roots level, to modernize Shari'a (Islamic law) and seeking internal Islamic resources for democracy, human rights, and, controversially, a secular state. Political discourse can generate change in the Muslim world, he believes, but only if it is done by Muslims, and only if it can draw on traditions rooted in Islamic and Arabic culture. Among his dozen books, the most important are *Toward an Islamic Revolution*, translated into Arabic, Farsi, Indonesian, and Russian, and *Islam and the Secular State: Negotiating the Future of Shari'a*, with Arabic, Bengali, French, Indonesian, and Urdu editions. He has lectured throughout the world, and with generous support from the Ford Foundation, he has led a series of Center projects on Islamic family law, Islam and human rights, and the future of Shari'a.

Michael J. Broyde
J.D., New York University
Professor of Law, Emory University
CSLR Senior Fellow

The work of the Center has forced me to reflect on my own tradition in a much broader analytic way—for example, when I was working on an article about the Jewish tradition on proselytism as compared to that of other religions. In a vacuum, the Jewish tradition is the center of its own conversation, so it looks normal. But from an interdisciplinary perspective, you have to ask, "Why is the Jewish tradition so different from all these others?"

CSLR Senior Fellow David Blumenthal calls Michael Broyde "the world's most gifted and innovative rabbinic scholar under the age of 50." It's not a surprising description, in light of Broyde's prominent work in law, religion, and science in the Jewish perspective; the reform of Jewish marriage and family law; comparative religious law; and Jewish law and ethics. Ordained as a rabbi by Yeshiva University, Broyde played a major leadership role in creating America's largest Jewish law court, the Bet Din of America, of which he is a member (dayan). He has published five books and more than 70 articles in various aspects of law and religion and Jewish law, and a number of articles in the area of federal courts.

The multidisciplinary perspective of the Center, Broyde says, lends substantial vitality to its work: "Our scholarly projects bring many different kinds of people around the table, and although the sum is better than all the parts, each of the parts is relevant in its own right." Some of Broyde's relevant contributions to recent projects are *Marriage, Sex and Family in Judaism* and *Marriage, Divorce and the Abandoned Wife in Jewish Law: A Conceptual Understanding of the Agunah Problems in America.* He is currently directing a series of Center projects on Jewish legal studies.

Timothy P. Jackson
Ph.D., Yale University
Associate Professor of Christian Ethics, Emory University
CSLR Senior Fellow

When I was working on The Morality of Adoption, *the Center's seminars taught me the irreplaceable value of open, interdisciplinary conversation. We'd been talking for hours about the adoption rights of would-be parents but knew that a central focus was missing. Then we had an epiphany: The real focus ought to be on the right to be adopted. Once we shifted our emphasis to the needs of children rather than the interests of adults, the book suddenly began to take shape. Even the language of rights, we realized, is outstripped by the primacy of talking about love, about charity for the needy. I couldn't have come to that insight any other way.*

When Jackson arrived on campus in 1995 he became a key player in the Law and Religion Program. He has been among the leading participants in six Center projects, and now—in a natural segue from his work on adoption—is directing the project on "The Best Love of the Child."

In numerous articles and several books, Jackson has focused his research on moral philosophy and theology (including medical ethics), especially the relationship between secular and Christian conceptions of truth, goodness, justice, freedom, and mercy. An astute conversation partner and lectern presence, he recently received national coverage for his ardent defense of religion in two standing-room-only debates on religious faith with writer Christopher Hitchens.

Michael J. Perry
J.D., Columbia University
Robert W. Woodruff Professor of Law,
Emory University
CSLR Senior Fellow

Why does a liberal democracy protect the right not just to religious belief, but to religious practice? Once you discern the best case for protecting that right, another question arises: Should a liberal democracy protect the right to moral practice as well? And if we have the right to moral freedom, what implications might that suggest with respect to same-sex marriage?

For Perry, who calls himself "a dissident Catholic," the habit of intellectual questioning developed early, in a family steeped in Irish Catholicism but hospitable to critical inquiry: "I've always been interested in questions of religion and meaning, questions of morality as it unfolds in politics and law."

Before coming to Emory, Perry was Howard J. Trienens Professor of Law at Northwestern University and the University Distinguished Chair in Law at Wake Forest University. A world-class scholar—writing on highly contentious legal and political issues—he has focused on American constitutional law, the proper role of religiously-grounded morality in American law and politics, and the morality of human rights. He has produced 10 major university press titles, including *Toward a Theory of Human Rights: Religion, Law, Courts* and *Under God? Religious Faith and Liberal Democracy*. Along the way, he has taught as a visiting professor and guest scholar at Yale Law School, the University of Tokyo School of Law, and Trinity College (Dublin) School of Law. Leader of the Center's projects on "Religion and Human Rights" and "Roundtable on New Books in Law and Religion," Perry has added a vital philosophical voice to the Center's projects and publications.

Philip L. Reynolds
Ph.D., University of Toronto
Aquinas Professor of Historical Theology, Emory University
CSLR Senior Fellow

Happiness is both a perennial topic and a currently fashionable one, and the relation between some of the current trends in positive psychology and the traditions in philosophy and theology are as yet unclear, so this is an opportune time to take stock and to focus on the topic. What most intrigues me about the "Pursuit of Happiness" project is the way it brings scientists, humanities scholars, and theologians around the same table. The "dialects" that we use in our respective professional worlds are so diverse that our meetings sometimes feel like Babel, or chaos; and some members are a little troubled by that; but it's an adventure. Moreover, the usual turf battles that go on within academic fields are completely irrelevant here, which is quite refreshing.

Perhaps no other scholar worldwide knows as much as Philip Reynolds about the first millennium Common Era literature on marriage and family—and it would be hard to find his peer in the knowledge of 12th- and 13th-century scholastics (especially Bonaventure and Thomas Aquinas). A quietly brilliant intellectual leader and textual critic, Reynolds is currently directing the Center's major five-year project on "The Pursuit of Happiness," which draws on a score of scholars from a dozen disciplines.

He has published numerous articles in leading journals of medieval thought, as the well as the recent books *To Have and To Hold: Marrying and Its Documentation in Western Christendom, 400-1600* and *Marriage in the Western Church: The Christianization of Marriage During Patristic Times and Early Medieval Periods.*

Johan D. van der Vyver
L.L.D., University of Pretoria
IT Cohen Professor of International Law and Human Rights, Emory University
CSLR Senior Fellow

I've always tended to be critical of the establishment—and, in apartheid South Africa, for good reason. When I came to the United States I also found much that can be criticized, notably in the field of church-state relations. I don't think that the U.S. Supreme Court has found a clear answer to the relationship between law and religion, because the present system proceeds on what I consider a false premise: the idea that law and religion can be separated.

Van der Vyver was working with human rights long before he heard about the dynamic cluster of scholars at Emory. In 1978, as dean and professor of law at Potchefstroom University in his native South Africa, he openly challenged the policies of the apartheid government. When asked to submit to censorship, he resigned from the university but continued his pioneering efforts to end apartheid and bring constitutional reform to his native country. In 2003, Potchefstroom acknowledged South Africa's dramatic change of heart by inviting Van der Vyver back to campus to receive the Honorary Doctor of Law degree.

Formerly a professor of law at the University of the Witwatersrand in Johannesburg, South Africa, Van der Vyver is a ranking expert on international human rights, jurisprudence, religious liberty, and the international criminal court. He has served as a fellow in the Human Rights Program of the Carter Center, and has published 15 books in Afrikaans and English, including *The Protection of Human Rights in South Africa,* and more than 300 articles. In collaboration with John Witte and Abdullahi An-Na'im, he has led major Center projects on "Religious Human Rights in Global Perspective," "The Problem and Promise of Proselytism in the New World Order," "Religious Freedom and its Limitations," and a new project, funded by the Luce Foundation, on "Law, Religion, and Human Rights in International Perspective."

LAW AND RELIGION: WHY?

It's a question some might call frivolous. Others might label it naive. A prescient few—like Jim Laney, Frank Alexander, Hal Berman, John Witte, and those who have come alongside—would see, waiting just below the surface of that question, another one, even more compelling: the deceptively simple *Why not?*

In the Center's work of bringing law and religion into productive dialogue and constructive alliance, what matters, finally, is not the numbers of books published, conferences held, projects undertaken, or even participants attracted.

The essential thing, the *sine qua non*, is the wide-open forum—the welcoming and asking, the sharp thinking, and frank talking—all of which spark the effort and the example of reaching, again and again, for the intriguing question that arises *next.*

Every child in the world will say, "That's *my* toy." That's property law. Every child in the world will say, "But you *promised* me." That's contract law. Any child will say, "It's not *my* fault. He hit me first." That's tort law. A child will say, too, "Daddy *said* I could." That's constitutional law.

Law comes from human nature. And every legal rule rests on a belief-system; it may not be a belief in God, but it's a belief in something. The world is coming together around these beliefs. For too long, we've emphasized our differences. We'd do better to look at beliefs we hold in common.

Harold J. Berman
Robert W. Woodruff Professor of Law, Emory University

IN THE MIDDLE

Spurred by their own convictions and by the vacuum of scholarship in the field of law and religion study, the program's founders delved into history, jurisprudence, religious practices, international concerns—and possibilities.

BIG PROJECTS, BIG QUESTIONS

The Center has led research during the last 25 years to answer these major questions:

- Christianity and Democracy: Friends or Foes?
- Religion and Human Rights: Necessary Allies?
- Pushing the Faith: Whose Rites Get Rights?
- Truths that Must Be Told: Whose Responsibility?
- Modern Islam: Can Constitutionalism Thrive?
- For Better, For Worse: By Whose Decree?
- The Mystery of Children: Who Should Keep Watch?

Much of the Center's work has been conceived as a series of multi-year research projects designed to forecast the big questions and to resource the future debates about the ways religion and law overlap, conflict, and interact. Each of these projects begins in rigorous conversation around a large table. Some 15 to 25 scholars from different fields and faiths come together regularly for several sessions to consider and critique prospective facets of a broad topic. Working collaboratively, the group crafts the project's methodology, main themes, and intended results. Then the project's directors commission a series of fresh, individual studies: sometimes these are articles that eventually form an anthology; sometimes they are monographs that result in a book series. As the project gets underway, these meetings morph into forums for presentation and close collective critique of each scholar's work in progress.

Over time, a multi-year project typically sprouts numerous books, articles, large international conferences, public lectures, news coverage, opinion pieces, and rosters of participants—to date, more than 1,600—representing universities, organizations, and public policy-makers the world over. It also spawns additional activities: "side projects" springing from one or more scholars' interest in a new but related direction.

CHRISTIANITY AND DEMOCRACY: FRIENDS OR FOES?

It was the tumultuous 1980s. The Berlin Wall had crumbled. Eastern Europe had been liberated. The Soviet Union was dissolving. African autocrats were flinching. Apartheid was fading. Latin American dictators were falling. Islam was emerging. Since 1973, 30 new democracies had been born. And democratic agitation had reached even Tiananmen Square.

Berlin Wall, 1989

Tom Stoddart Collection/ Getty Images

At Emory, the law and religion scholars had been watching the drama of democracy. What's more, they were starting to shape it, by calling attention to the role of a central but little-noticed character: the Christian church. They raised questions: *How has Christianity already influenced this centuries-old drama? What can it—and should it—contribute in the future?* One question spanned all the others: *Are democracy and Christianity friends or foes?* In light of world events, that question couldn't have been more timely.

The Emory group was ready to launch its first international research project, "Christianity and Democracy in Global Context," examining many facets of the checkered relationship between these two conspicuous institutions. Harold Berman had already opened this new avenue of scholarship with his study of the Western legal tradition. (See "From Projects to Publications," page 34.)

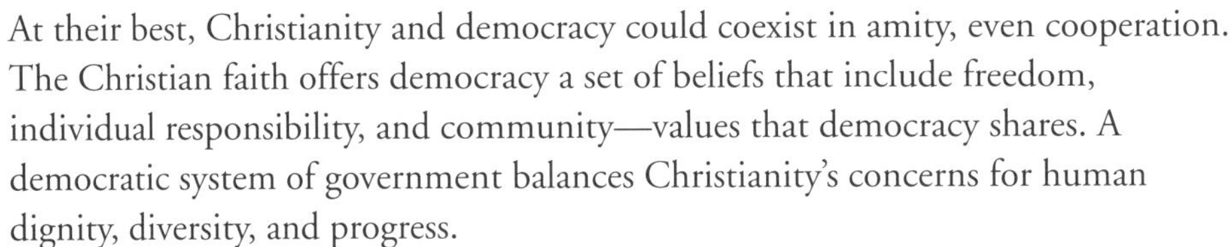

At their best, Christianity and democracy could coexist in amity, even cooperation. The Christian faith offers democracy a set of beliefs that include freedom, individual responsibility, and community—values that democracy shares. A democratic system of government balances Christianity's concerns for human dignity, diversity, and progress.

And like genuine friends, the two can take each other to task. Democracy might say to the church: *Practice what you preach. Don't give lip service to liberty and equality while supporting patriarchal and hierarchical conditions inside the church walls.*

Christianity, in turn, challenges democracy: *Among political forms, you're the world's best hope. Extend yourself. Reform yourself. Stop impoverishing the already poor and exploiting the already exploited while promising them a better life.*

But perfect collaboration between democracy and Christianity is an ideal. In reality, both systems are flawed and inconsistent. And neither lends itself to simple interpretation.

Leading the project, John Witte, Jr., asked some 50 scholars from around the globe, "What have Christian ideas and institutions contributed to the modern democratic revolution of the world? How has Christianity interacted with democracy in the countries you know best?"

The project culminated in a major international conference, "Christianity and Democracy in Global Context" and a book of the same title, edited by Witte. Later it also informed several other titles, including Witte's prize-winning volume, *Law and Protestantism: The Legal Teachings of the Lutheran Reformation.* (See "From Projects to Publications," page 34.)

WELCOME • CHRISTIANITY • DEMOCRACY

For four days in November 1991, some 800 scholars, lawyers, theologians, clergy, and laypersons from five continents—along with media representatives from near and far—converged on Atlanta to attend Emory's conference, "Christianity and Democracy in Global Context." They were bent on bringing to light some tough questions that, from their own lived experience, they individually and collectively found imperative:

What roles has Christianity played in democratic movements throughout the world?

How is Christian thought influencing democracy even now?

To what extent—and in what ways—can the interplay between democracy and Christianity benefit global society?

From left: Jim Laney, Marcos McGrath, Jimmy Carter, Josef Smolik (University of Prague), and John Witte, 1991

I think we have approached a point where we can prove whether it is possible to exhibit simultaneously the Christian characteristics of compassion, of sharing, and of peace with the democratic principles of freedom, equality, human rights, and the right of the people to rule.

Former U.S. President Jimmy Carter
Christianity and Democracy in Global Context

Former U.S. President Jimmy Carter opened the conference, urging participants to be realistic in their recognition of world problems, yet at the same time offering optimism: "There is no more Cold War. We have an open slate to describe the future."

Next, more than 40 distinguished authorities from around the world debated the contributions of Christianity to democratic ideas and institutions in their respective homelands. Protestants and Catholics, Africans and Americans, freedom fighters and prime ministers shared the same stage and shared their own stories. This event, the first major international conference sponsored by the Law and Religion Program, assembled and whetted viewpoints on conditions in Latin America, Europe, North America, and Africa.

Desmond Tutu and Marcos McGrath, 1991

We as Christians should also know that we cannot produce a constitutional blueprint which can be stamped as Christian par excellence. We can say that there is a broad spectrum of options ranging from those barely enshrining the values of the kingdom of God to those which most nearly embody those values and principles.

Desmond M. Tutu
Anglican Archbishop of Cape Town, South Africa
Christianity and Democracy in Global Context

Some of the viewpoints recorded in *Emory Report* on December 9, 1991:

Latin America. Years of instability at the hands of military regimes have left the poor suspicious of democracy, according to Marcos McGrath, Roman Catholic Archbishop of Panama.

Eastern Europe. "Democracy was once a dirty word. It's now a problem for politicians [to know] how to speak, how to explain the situation," said Lazlo Surjan, Hungary's Minister of Welfare.

Africa. Emory Political Science Professor Richard Joseph urged African churches to stand up to oppressive regimes: "We are an active force for human rights, for democratic rights ..."

North America. United Nations Ambassador Andrew Young said he couldn't accept democracy as defined in North America when he was a young boy and society was segregated along racial lines. Yet, in his view, democracy empowers people to break down the walls that divide them.

Anglican Archbishop Desmond Tutu of Cape Town, South Africa, closed the conference to a capacity crowd of 1,200 at the Cathedral of St. Philip in Atlanta. It is not in isolation but through community that we define our humanity, he said, adding, "God has made us different so that we can realize our need of one another. And so the truly democratic state would let people celebrate their rich diversity."

It was a conference to set the standard—and it did.

THE MEDIA'S COMMENTARY

Carter: End 'discrimination by rich against poor'

Former president urges government, church to do more

By Elizabeth Kurylo
STAFF WRITER

Former President Jimmy Carter challenged hundreds of clerics, scholars and political leaders from around the world to reach out to the needy with compassion and to bridge the chasm between rich and poor.

"The greatest discrimination

▶ Emory forum focuses on Christianity and democracy. **A12**

dropouts or drug addiction, juvenile delinquency or homelessness or unemployment.

"We preach to each other, we deal with each other, we minister to each other when next door, or around the world, the needs are unmet," Mr. Carter said.

"I'm not here to criticize others. I'm part of it," said Mr. Carter, adding that he has only recently started to learn about Atlanta's poor.

Three weeks ago, Mr. Carter announced an ambitious project to attack intractable social problems ranging from the homeless to delinquency and drug abuse.

He repeated his call for Atlanta's churches to join in his project, saying that "tens of thousands" of volunteers are needed.

When Mr. Carter announced the Atlanta Project, he said that much of the work would depend on volunteers, especially from churches. He added that despite good intentions, churches are "basically a dormant element of self-gratification and security."

NEWS The Atlanta Journal / The Atlanta Constitution

Tutu takes the church to task

Record assailed on human rights

By Cynthia Durcanin
STAFF WRITER

South African Archbishop Desmond M. Tutu concluded an international conference on Christianity and democracy Sunday with harsh words for the church and its mixed track record on human rights.

"We do not have a monopoly on wisdom and most certainly not on morality and righteousness," the Anglican Archbishop told a crowd of 1,200 at the Cathedral of St. Philip Episcopal on Peachtree Road.

"It is devastating to think that the obscenity and horror of the Holocaust, which must remain one of the crowning shames of the Christian era, was perpetrated not by pagans wallowing in the thick darkness of unbelief and superstition."

Sharp words: Archbishop Desm… Christians" Sunday at the Cathec…

The Atlanta Journal / The Atlanta Constitution · Sunday, November 17, 1991 **B1**

CHRISTIANITY AND DEMOCRACY

African faithful urged to support democracy

'Voice of church has to be heard'

By Elizabeth Kurylo
STAFF WRITER

Churches in Africa must embrace human rights as part of their mission if they want to help fledgling democratic movements succeed, an aide to former President Jimmy Carter said Saturday at an international conference on Christianity and democracy.

"The churches have a role to play," said Richard Joseph, an expert on African studies at the Carter Center of Emory University. "The voice of the church has to be heard from the beginning."

Churches in Africa have often been complacent about oppressive dictatorial governments, and in some cases helped those governments, Dr. Joseph said.

"They have not actually seen themselves as mandated to have an environment in which human rights and free expression was the order of the day," Dr. Joseph said. "That is something that just comes along tangentially."

He challenged African churches to stand up to repressive regimes and say, "We are an active force for human rights, for democratic rights, and we are for those objectives all the time."

Dr. Joseph said African nations are going through a "second independence" movement and that churches have a vital role in helping it succeed.

When African nations were dominated by European colonial rulers, the governments "looked up to most religious bodies as allies and as agents in the establishment of their dominance," he said.

When those governments were replaced by oppressive authoritarian regimes, the churches were mostly silent. "The churches were carrying on their business for very long periods," he said.

Nevertheless, said Kwame Bediako, director of the Akrofi-Christaller Memorial Centre in Ghana, Christianity has had a significant impact in moving nations toward democracy.

"It is doubtful whether those nations of the world which have developed lasting traditions of authentic democratic political arrangements would have done so without a sustained and protracted Christian presence and impact within them."

Today, "church leaders are coming forward in the transition period" away from authoritarian regimes, Dr. Joseph said. If they continue to speak out for basic human rights, they can help democracy take root in Africa.

Scholars and church leaders from throughout Africa attended the conference and offered differing views on the church's history and role.

"The church is the only voice of dissent in many African countries," said Sulaiman Z. Jakonda, executive director of the Rural Development Counsellors for Christian Churches in Africa in Jos, Nigeria.

Yet, he said, "the church needs to do much more than protest. It can organize and help people to know their rights and not to sell their voting card for a potage of bean soup."

South Africa was cited as an example where some churches "allowed themselves to be used in ungodly ways" to promote apartheid, said Johan van der Vyver, a South African human rights activist and scholar.

In South Africa, such religious leaders as Anglican Archbishop Desmond Tutu have been the exception, not the rule, in the fight against apartheid, Dr. van der Vyver said.

Another South Africa scholar, Charles Villa-Vicencio, said that in order for South Africa to make a true break from its racist past, the nation must offer a national apology.

"The nation has to put the lights on and admit the extent to which" it discriminated against blacks, he said.

Richard Joseph challenges African churches to stand up to repressive regimes.

Charles Villa-Vicencio says South Africa must break from its racist past, offer a national apology.

▶ Whence Christianity, now that it has survived communism? **B4**
▶ Andrew Young: Duke a hit because poor whites feel "left behind" **B2**

Christianity, democracy enjoying new harmony
This international gathering seems dedicated to the hopeful proposition that Christianity is good for democracy, and vice versa. It is a relatively new proposition.
(*Atlanta Journal-Constitution,* November 16, 1991)

Christianity survived communism, but where does it go from here?
A principal concern of the Emory conference on Christianity and democracy has been how to ensure that democratic society is animated by values more noble than the pursuit of self-interest.
(*Atlanta Journal-Constitution,* November 17, 1991)

Tutu takes the church to task
South African Archbishop Desmond M. Tutu concluded an international conference on Christianity and democracy Sunday with harsh words for the church and its mixed track record on human rights. ... "We do not have a monopoly on wisdom and most certainly not on morality and righteousness," the Anglican Archbishop told a crowd of 1,200 at the Cathedral of St. Philip Episcopal on Peachtree Road.
(*Atlanta Journal-Constitution,* November 18, 1991)

FROM PROJECTS TO PUBLICATIONS

The Center's research on Christianity and democracy has asked in various ways, *The Christian church and the system of democracy, constitutional order, and rule of law: What do they share? How do they support each other, work against each other, and, in the process, evolve?*

PROJECTS

The Western Legal Tradition (1987 -)
An analysis of the formation and periodic transformation of the Western legal tradition under the influence of revolutionary new belief-systems, and the transition toward the formation of a new world law in the new millennium.
Highlights: seven books

Law, Religion, and the Protestant Tradition (1998 -)
A systematic analysis of the historical contributions of mainline Protestantism, particularly Calvinism, to the development of the Western law of marriage, family, and children, and of rights, liberties, and constitutionalism.
Highlights: five books

Christian Jurisprudence (1999 -)
A comprehensive investigation of the contributions of modern Catholic, Protestant, and Orthodox figures to fundamental questions of law, politics, and society.
Highlights: three-volume book, 30 volumes commissioned

SELECTED PUBLICATIONS

Harold J. Berman, *Law and Revolution: The Formation of the Western Legal Tradition* (Harvard University Press, 1983) (with Chinese, French, German, Japanese, Polish, Portuguese, Russian, and Spanish translations)
Where did our modern Western legal institutions and concepts come from? Breaking new ground in legal history, Berman traces them back nine centuries to the Papal Revolution—an upheaval in which the Western church established its independence from emperors, kings, and feudal lords. Over centuries the Western idea of integrated legal systems consciously developed, including canon law, royal law, urban law, feudal law, manorial law, and mercantile law.

John Witte, Jr., *The Reformation of Rights: Law, Religion, and Human Rights in the Calvinist Tradition* (Cambridge University Press, 2007)
Challenging both Karl Barth's deprecation of Calvinist natural law theory and Leo Strauss's exaggeration of Enlightenment rights talk, Witte shows that early modern Calvinism was one of the driving engines of Western constitutionalism, influencing modern Western understandings of civil and political rights, social and confessional pluralism, federalism and social contract, and more.

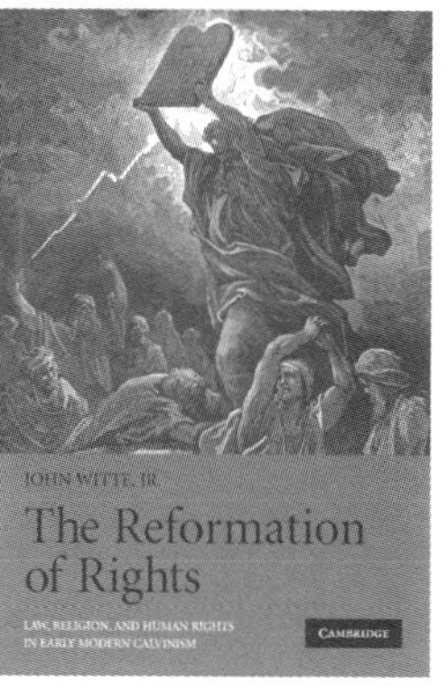

John Witte, Jr. and Frank S. Alexander, eds., *The Teachings of Modern Christianity on Law, Politics, and Human Nature* (Columbia University Press, 2005-2007), 2 vols., 3 vols. paperback
It's all here: writings from the most important Christian thinkers of the 19th and 20th centuries, along with extensive biographical and bibliographical information, and a wide-ranging analysis of these thinkers' work by leading scholars. The collection underscores how these crucial figures have shaped and continue to shape current debates about the family, state, religion, and society, the nature and purpose of law and authority, the limits of rule and obedience, the care and nurture of the needy and innocent, the rights and wrongs of war and violence, and the separation of church and state.

Harold J. Berman, *Faith and Order: The Reconciliation of Law and Religion* (Wm. B. Eerdmans, 1993)

Harold J. Berman, et al., *The Nature and Functions of Law,* 6th ed. (Foundation Press, 2004)

Harold J. Berman, *Law and Revolution II: The Impact of the Protestant Reformation on the Western Legal Tradition* (Harvard University Press, 2003)

Howard O. Hunter, ed., *The Integrative Jurisprudence of Harold J. Berman* (Westview Press, 1996)

John Witte, Jr., ed., *Christianity and Democracy in Global Context* (Westview Press, 1993)

John Witte, Jr., *Law and Protestantism: The Legal Teachings of the Lutheran Reformation* (Cambridge University Press, 2002)

John Witte, Jr., *God's Joust, God's Justice: Law and Religion in Western History* (Wm. B. Eerdmans, 2006)

John Witte, Jr., and Frank S. Alexander, eds., *Cambridge Companion to Law and Christianity* (Cambridge University Press, forthcoming)

A complete listing of projects and books is available at www.law.emory.edu/cslr.

There is a lesson we have learned in Panama, Nicaragua, and elsewhere ... Democracy is not simply a garment to be put on at will. ... Democracy, in all its dimensions, requires education, formation, and motivation at every level.

Marcos McGrath, C.S.C.
Christianity and Democracy in Global Context

It seems to me to take a special kind of arrogance to confront the other regions of the world with the beneficent as well as the disastrous consequences of technology and industrialization, but at the same time to declare them incapable of a proper understanding of democracy and human rights.

Wolfgang Huber
Lutheran Bishop of Berlin-Brandenburg
Christianity and Democracy in Global Context

Has Christianity been a force to advance justice, or has it been more of a drag on "progress"?

The APJ Beat, November 1990
The Center for Public Justice
Washington, D.C.

WHAT ABOUT HUMAN RIGHTS?

To the question *Christianity and democracy: friends or foes?* no consensus of views emerged. But Witte points out in *Christianity and Democracy in Global Context* that democracy needs Christianity. "Democracy needs ... opposition to survive. For democracy ... presupposes the existence of a body of beliefs and values that will constantly shape and reshape it. ... With the long tradition of theological and philosophical reflection on democracy at its disposal, Christianity cannot be silent."

A number of persistent patterns characterize the past encounters between Christianity and democracy, and a number of common challenges face them in cultures throughout the world.

One of those challenges became critically apparent during the conference sessions. Repeatedly, speakers pointed to individual human dignity as a quality to which Christianity and democracy alike owe support. The topic of the program's next major project and conference evolved as a matter of course.

RELIGION AND HUMAN RIGHTS: NECESSARY ALLIES?

The topic of religious human rights began percolating at the Center's international conference on Christianity and democracy in 1991. Research and conversations had illuminated the overall problem: Religious human rights had become, in the phrase of Ninth Circuit Court of Appeals Judge John Noonan, "a neglected stepchild of the human rights movement."

In 1993, 25 scholars from Western Europe, Israel, South Africa, Central America, and the United States gathered at Emory to delve into the issue. Johan D. van der Vyver, a leading scholarly proponent for constitutional and human rights reform in his native South Africa, opened the discussion: "The traditional neglect of religious human rights in the academies and in the activist communities of the world has had deleterious consequences for the field of human rights. It has impoverished contemporary discourse about human rights as a whole. It has sharpened the divide between Western and non-Western theories and understandings of rights. It has contributed to the abstraction of current understandings of rights, particularly popular understandings. And it has introduced considerable distortions in both the learning and the activity related to religious human rights."

Examples taking place around the world were compiled by Daniel G. Ashburn, a graduate of Emory's Law and Religion Program:

Kenya. Government seizure of Christian publications, and the expelling of 1,300 refugees who were receiving assistance from an Islamic aid organization

Croatia. Serious human rights abuses perpetrated against Muslims, including property damage, harassment and threats, and denial of citizenship

France. Forbidding students to wear religious symbols in the public schools; four Muslim schoolgirls expelled for wearing headscarves

Guatemala. Reports of religious officials being threatened, harassed, and even killed for political reasons

Pakistan. Law making blasphemy against the prophet Mohammed—or his family or companions—a capital offense

The roundtable discussion yielded six core themes to be pursued in a budding project, "Religious Human Rights in Global Perspective": 1) historical, conceptual, methodological approaches to religion and human rights; 2) religious foundations of human rights; 3) human rights foundations of religious freedom; 4) international, regional, and national laws on religious freedom; 5) religion and human rights in situations of political transition; and 6) the place of rights within religious communities and religious legal systems.

The world community deals with religion because it is there and will not go away. ...To believe that one can deal with issues of rights while neglecting religion is to lose power to deal with most human beings.

Martin E. Marty
University of Chicago
Religious Human Rights in Global Perspective

Scholars returned to their institutions prepared to explore their individual slices of the issue. The plan: to zoom out from the earlier focus on Christianity to include "the four corners of the Book"—Judaism, Islam, Catholicism, and Protestant Christianity—and simultaneously to zoom in on religious human rights in "the four corners of the Atlantic"—Latin America, North America, Europe, and Africa.

John Witte, who co-directed the project with Van der Vyver, summed up the group's goal: "The driving engine behind this project is to take stock of what has been done—and what should be done—in both the activist and scholarly communities, and to bring both groups together for a major body of work."

Religion and human rights: are they necessary allies? The gathered scholars had emerged from the roundtable with a shared perspective on that question: *Religions are not easy allies to engage. But the struggle for human rights cannot be won without them.*

It is time for us to take religious rights seriously —to shake off our political indifference and parochial self-interest and to address the plight and protection of people of all faiths.

"Religious Human Rights in the World Today" conference program

THE CONFERENCE: TIMELY AND VITAL

By fall 1994, seven roundtables had convened around the world. Project participants were prepared to talk about the issues publicly, and people were ready to listen. More than 750 academicians, activists, and religious leaders from around the world, along with many Emory students and the public at large, gathered on the Emory campus for a major international conference, "Religious Human Rights in the World Today."

Luminaries Archbishop Desmond M. Tutu, the University of Chicago's Martin E. Marty, and Judge John Noonan served as keynote speakers. Noonan said in his address:

"The foundation of religious rights is found in the human conscience, that capability of every human being to tell right from wrong. How do the special characteristics of conscience convert into moral rights? In two ways. To force anyone to act against conscience is to force that person to act against that person's reason and so against that person's nature. ... The second reason is, for any believer in God, stronger still. To command anyone to perform an action against conscience is ... to violate that person's duty of obedience to God."

Desmond Tutu (right) with Johan van der Vyer (left) and Emory President William M. Chase, 1994

The numerous plenary and in-depth concurrent sessions explored religious human rights under four broad headings: Foundations, Religious Dimensions, Legal Dimensions, and Integration of Religious Human Rights. Fifty speakers presented papers on topics close to their individual hearts: activism for religious rights; the rights of women, children, and dissidents; religious rights in various regions of the world; and the testimony of religious texts for Judaism, Christianity, and Islam.

Selected comments:

"Currently Bosnia and Herzegovina are hell, and in hell there are no religious human rights," said Paul Mojzes, professor of religion at Rosemont College.

An assessment of religious human rights in Latin America came from Paul Sigmund, professor of politics and director of the Latin American Studies Program at Princeton University: "There are still hurdles to be overcome ... but the principal battles for religious liberty have been won, although only in recent times. The outlook for religious human rights in Latin America is the one of guarded optimism."

Participants' focuses ranged from the widespread history of religious rights abuses to new evidence of progress and even to the hope that a worldwide law on freedom of religion for all might actually be possible.

World scholars join Emory talks on religious liberty in the '90s

By Gayle White
STAFF WRITER

It's an old story: Through brute force, one religious group forces its views on another ethnic or religious faction.

It happened during the Crusades, which began in the 11th century. It happened after several republics broke away from Yugoslavia in the 1990s.

"Currently Bosnia and Herzegovina is hell, and in hell there are no religious human rights," says Paul Mojzes, professor of religious studies at Rosemont College and editor of Religion in Eastern Europe.

Mojzes is one of 50 scholars in Atlanta this weekend for an international conference on religious rights that is being sponsored by Emory University.

In most areas of the world, the battle over religion is not nearly as obvious as in some Balkan nations, where people are being raped, killed, imprisoned or exiled because of their ethnic or religious identity.

In fact, worldwide the recognition of religious rights is expanding as never before, according to the scholars. But when it comes to the actual practice, there is still tension between

Progress, setbacks for worshipers

The state of religious freedom in Africa, Europe, and North and South America, as reported by scholars meeting

The root of all human rights

The cry for rights — privacy rights, animal rights, consumer rights and so on — can sometimes seem a swelling cacophony of self-interest.

A four-day international conference in Atlanta that concludes today helps bring harmony out of the noise by sounding the deep organ tones underneath all rights — the right to freedom of religion.

In our secular cities, religious rights tend to get lost among more chic concerns. Last year's passage of the Religious Freedom Restoration Act, a bipartisan bill backed by an unprecedented coalition of religious groups large and small, barely registered in the media.

Religious rights — the claim of a freedom of conscience — are primary among all rights, which is why religious freedom begins the Bill of Rights. The theme of the conference convened by Emory University is that religious rights are also the source of other rights — to assemble, speak, teach, publish, parent or travel. They should be accorded their proper place, scholars said, as democracy spreads from Eastern Europe to South Africa.

"There's no political manifesto that is as radical as the Bible. . . . It's exciting, very exhilarating, to be a believer."

ARCHBISHOP DESMOND TUTU

Connecting today's revolutions with religion suggests a breathtaking, dramatic story. Jean Bethke Elshtain, one of the scholars at the conference, describes the classical Greek and Roman world as one in which the state made an absolute claim on human bodies — males as warriors, females as breeders. The Judeo-Christian dissent from this was a revolutionary claim of individual privacy, sacredness, choice. In many ways, that revolution continues today.

It is hard to imagine, for example, how a non-racial democracy could have come about in South Africa without people who were motivated by their understanding of scripture.

"There's no political manifesto that is as radical as the Bible," said South African Archbishop Desmond Tutu, in Atlanta to kick off the conference. "It's exciting, very exhilarating, to be a believer," said the affable Nobel laureate.

To describe what is happening in South Africa, he said, "even non-religious people find they must use religious language."

Amen.

Tutu hails South Africa's healing

Anglican Archbishop Desmond Tutu of Cape Town, South Africa, gave the keynote address Thursday night at a major international religious rights conference sponsored by Emory University.

Desmond Tutu

THE MEDIA'S COMMENTARY

The conference raised public awareness of religious human rights violations. From the *Atlanta Journal-Constitution*, October 9, 1994:

> PROGRESS, SETBACKS FOR WORSHIPERS
>
> The state of religious freedom in Africa, Europe, and North and South America, as reported by scholars meeting this weekend at Emory University:
>
> *Africa:* There is a heightened concern for religious fundamentalism within a pluralistic culture that includes Islam, Christianity, animism, and even forms of ancestor worship. In Algeria, Egypt, and Sudan, there is tension over activities of Islamic fundamentalists.
>
> *South Africa:* A transitional constitution broadly entrenches religious rights and freedoms, but the full consequences have not been realized. Experts expect challenges, especially to those provisions that seem to have a Christian bias. This is one place on the African continent where Christian fundamentalism has been culturally dominant in the past.

Balkan countries: Because of close ties between ethnicity and religion, wars since 1991 have resulted in the destruction of sacred buildings, the execution of religious leaders, and the obstruction of religious services.

India: With no common civil code governing marriage, divorce, adoption, and inheritance, each religious group within India continues to control crucial aspects of people's lives—especially those of women—denying them effective citizenship and civil rights.

Latin America: Religious rights are better guaranteed than ever in Latin America, except in Cuba and Haiti. Evangelical Protestants and Pentecostals are more active in the region, but tensions continue between the dominant Roman Catholic Church and minority religious groups.

United States: After the U.S. Supreme Court held in 1990 that religious practices could be curtailed by neutral laws, late last year Congress passed and President Clinton signed the Religious Freedom Restoration Act, which ensures a higher standard of review in religious liberty cases.

Soon afterward, an article in the *Christian Science Monitor* opened with a list of harsh details:

"The 'ethnic cleansing' of Muslims in Bosnia. Clashes between Sikkhs and Hindus in India. The bitter strife between Catholics and Protestants in Northern Ireland. And in the U.S., the denial of permission for Jews to build synagogues or Muslims to construct mosques in some neighborhoods. From one corner of the globe to another, religious worshipers are being killed, tortured, dislocated, or denied liberties because of their beliefs." (October 19, 1994)

Religion is an ineradicable condition of human persons and communities.

Religions invariably provide universal sources and scales of values by which many persons and communities govern and measure themselves.

Religions invariably suffuse the cultural, ethnic, and national identity of a person and a people.

Religions must thus be seen as indispensable allies in the modern struggle for human rights and democratization.

John Witte, Jr.
Religious Human Rights in Global Perspective

THE RESULTS: EXPANSIVE AND POTENT

The project's wide reach inspired a surge of new scholarship that continues today, initiating inquiries and conversations that had been conspicuously absent for far too long. (See "From Projects to Publications," page 42.)

Why had religious rights not been taken seriously in the early 1990s when the Law and Religion Program began its project? Why had this basic human freedom gone largely uninvestigated? Ignorance leads the long list of reasons, both because activist and academic communities often failed to communicate effectively and because media reports tended to feature more sensational instances of abuse that claimed more immediate attention.

To oppress [people], to trample their dignity underfoot, is not just evil, not just painful. ... It is positively blasphemous, for it is tantamount to spitting in the face of God.

Desmond M. Tutu
"Religious Human Rights in the World Today" conference address

---

[W]e recognize that many atrocities have been and continue to be committed in the name of God. Because religion can be such a powerful force for good and evil, the protection of religious rights becomes critically important.

Jimmy Carter
Religious Human Rights in Global Perspective

Religion, however private, is to many people the most critical aspect of life. And religious rights, however convoluted and controversial, must be addressed. For religious rights are the wellspring of many other rights: the rights of persons to assemble, speak, teach, publish, parent, or travel based upon their beliefs; and the rights of religious groups to govern themselves, worship collectively, own corporate property, organize charity, and practice political advocacy. To neglect religious rights is to cut other individual and group rights from their historical and conceptual source.

Such a sundering is what the Center's project ardently sought to prevent.

FROM PROJECTS TO PUBLICATIONS

The emerging field of religious human rights abounds with possible directions for new study. Big gaps in existing research have combined with the individual interests of particular CSLR senior fellows to create ongoing lines of exploration.

PROJECTS

Cultural Transformation in Africa: Legal, Theological, and Human Rights Perspectives (1996 - 2003)
An exploration of cultural transformation in Africa, with particular emphasis on the improvement of women's rights to and control over land as a vital economic resource and vindication of second-generation rights.
Highlights: roundtable conferences in Atlanta and Cape Town, South Africa; two books

Religious Liberty in Russia (1993 - 1997)
Analysis of the eroding protections of religious liberty in post-glasnost Russia, particularly for religious minorities and foreign faiths.
Highlights: roundtable conference in the Netherlands; two journal symposia

Religious Freedom and Limitations Clauses in International and Constitutional Law (2003 - 2006)
A comparative legal analysis of limitation clauses in international law and in selected countries in Europe and the Americas.
Highlights: regional conferences in Atlanta, Trier, Budapest, and Strasbourg; two journal symposia

Roundtables on New Books on Law, Religion, and Human Rights (2005 -)
Close collective discussion of drafts of new books in the field by Abdullahi An-Na'im, Timothy P. Jackson, Michael J. Perry, and Nicholas P. Wolterstorff.

Foundations and Frontiers of Religious Liberty (2005 - 2007)
A comparative analysis of the state of religious liberty in selected countries as part of the 25th anniversary celebration of the United Nations Declaration on Religious Intolerance and Discrimination Based Upon Religion and Belief.
Highlights: roundtable conferences in Atlanta; journal symposium

Law, Religion, and Human Rights in International Perspective (2007 -)
An updated comprehensive study of the state of religion and human rights in the world today, featuring conferences, interviews, new media resources, and white papers on the future of study in this field.

SELECTED PUBLICATIONS

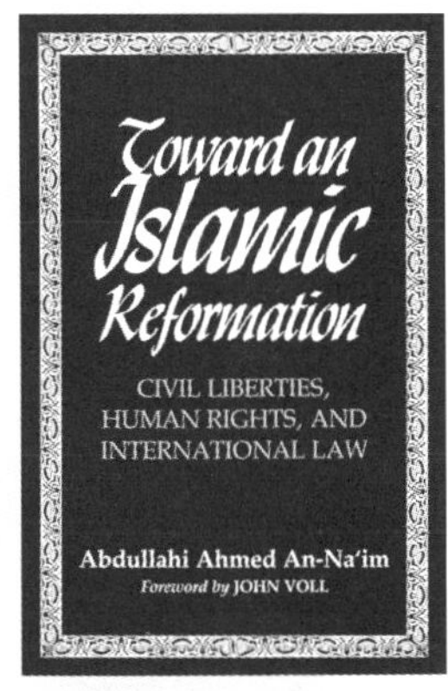

Abdullahi Ahmed An-Na'im, *Toward an Islamic Reformation: Civil Liberties, Human Rights and International Law* (Syracuse University Press, 1990)
Arising from An-Na'im's personal experiences as a Muslim from Northern Sudan struggling to reconcile his Islamic faith and identity with his commitment to universal acceptance of and respect for human rights, this book develops a modernist reformulation of Shari'a (the normative system of Islam) that is consistent with international human rights standards.

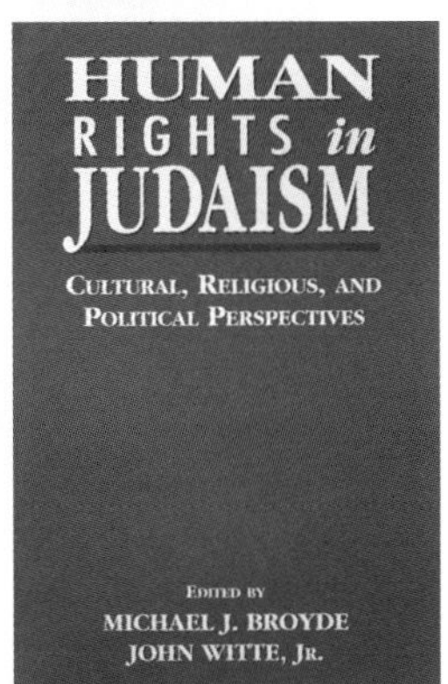

Michael J. Broyde and John Witte, Jr., eds., *Human Rights in Judaism: Cultural, Religious and Political Perspectives* (Jason Aronson Publishers, 1998)
Written by some of the most highly regarded scholars in the field, this collection of essays examines the remarkable contributions that Judaism has made, and can make, to the theory, law, and activism of human rights. It paints a vivid picture of how the Jewish tradition teaches its followers to respect the sanctity of every individual and to save many "worlds" through the preservation of human rights.

Michael J. Perry, *Toward a Theory of Human Rights: Religion, Law, Courts* (Cambridge University Press, 2007)
Making a significant contribution both to human rights studies and to constitutional theory, Perry addresses three tough questions: Is there a non-religious (secular) ground for the morality of human rights? What is the relation between the morality of human rights and the law of human rights? In a liberal democracy, what is the proper role of courts in protecting—and therefore in interpreting—human rights that are constitutionally entrenched?

Johan D. van der Vyver, *Leuven Lectures on Religious Institutions, Religious Communities, and Rights* (Peeters, 2004)

Van der Vyver discusses the principle of "sphere sovereignty" that marks the relationship between religious institutions and the state. He considers religious institutions both as organizational structures and thus distinct entities in human society, and also as legal persons that are repositories of rights and obligations. Religious communities, in contrast, comprise persons sharing the same confession of faith; since they lack an organizational structure, they do not qualify for legal subjectivity. Instead, rights associated with such a community belong to its individual members.

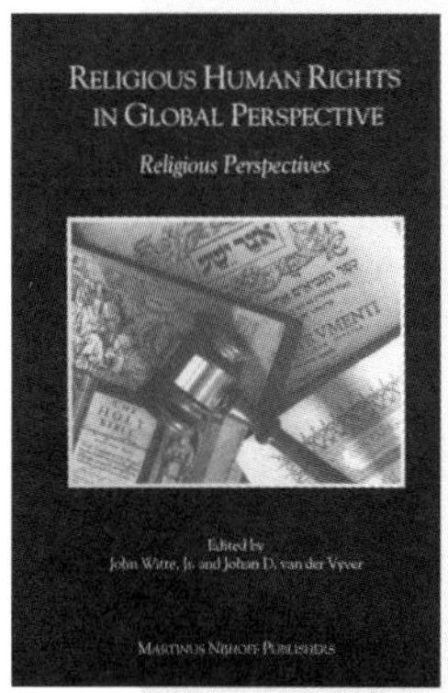

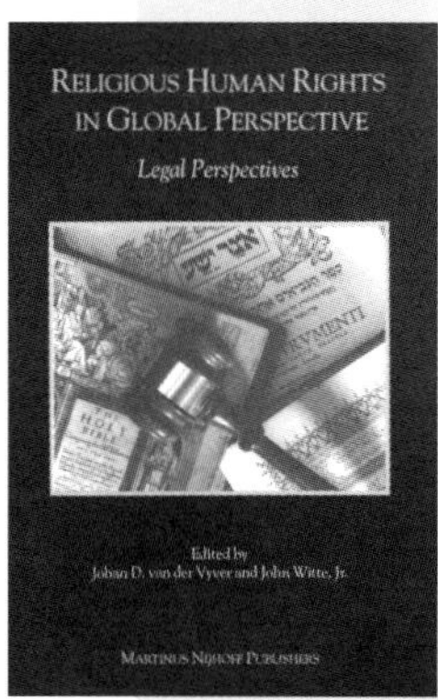

John Witte, Jr. and Johan D. van der Vyver, eds., *Religious Human Rights in Global Perspective* (Martinus Nijhoff, 1996), 2 vols.

The world has cultivated the best of religious rights protections but still witnesses the worst of religious rights abuses. These paired books, born of the 1994 conference "Religious Human Rights in the World Today," deliver a spectrum of knowledge and experience. The first volume offers religious perspective on religious rights, focusing on the teachings and practices of the three religions of the Book. In volume two, Jimmy Carter, John Noonan, Jr., and a score of leading jurists assess critically and comparatively the religious rights laws and practices in selected nations and regions on the four Atlantic continents. The work has become one of the anchor texts of religion and human rights study around the world, and portions have been translated into French, German, Italian, Romanian, Russian, Spanish, and Ukrainian.

Abdullahi Ahmed An-Na'im, ed., *Cultural Transformation and Human Rights in Africa* (Zed Books, 2002)

T. Jeremy Gunn, *Cultural Constraints and Historical Legacies: The Legal Regulation of Religion in Ten Countries* (forthcoming)

T. Jeremy Gunn, *Religion and United States Foreign Policy* (Praeger Press, forthcoming)

Natan Lerner, *Religion, Belief, and International Human Rights* (Orbis Books, 2000)

Michael J. Perry, *Under God? Religious Faith and Liberal Democracy* (Cambridge University Press, 2003)

Michael J. Perry, *The Idea of Human Rights: Four Inquiries* (Oxford University Press, 2000)

Symposium, "The State of Religious Human Rights in the World Today," *Emory International Law Review* 10 (1996): 52-186, with translations in *Conscience et liberté* 51 (1996): 18-120; *Coscienza e Libertà* 27 (1996): 47-191; *Gewissen und Freiheit* 46/47 (1996): 24-176

Symposium, "The Permissible Scope of Legal Limitations on the Freedom of Religion or Belief," *Emory International Law Review* 19 (2005): 465-1320

Symposium, "The Foundations and Frontiers of Religious Liberty," *Emory International Law Review* 21 (2007): 1-275

L. Muthoni Wanyeki, ed., *Women and Land in Africa: Culture, Religion, and Realizing Women's Rights* (Zed Books, 2003)

A complete listing of projects and books is available at www.law.emory.edu/cslr.

A GOLDEN RULE: POSSIBLE?

None of the three religions of the Book speaks unequivocally about human rights, and none has amassed an exemplary human rights record over the centuries. In this respect, Judaism, Islam, and Christianity all stand at the same starting line in the effort to protect religious rights.

Religion and human rights may indeed prove necessary allies, but ahead lies the need for an even more difficult alliance: a new bond of understanding among religious traditions. The Center's project on Religion and Human Rights urges religious groups to come together not only to listen and to converse—itself a major achievement—but to develop "Golden Rules of Religious Liberty" prescribing that as religious people, we all treat each other in the way we ourselves would like to be treated.

"We have struck a need in this project in ways we hadn't anticipated," said Van der Vyver. "Everybody has confirmed the need for much more concerned academic reflection on religious rights discourse."

One of the unanticipated results of the project, in fact, was a new idea for the project to consider. In 1994, the *Wesleyan Christian Advocate* reported Witte's statement of three reasons why one religious group feels compelled to oppress another: "zealous belief in one's own faith and the desire to convert others; the protection of one's faith group from outside influence; and the presence of sin, which allows one group to believe it is more sacred than another." (October 21, 1994)

John S. Pobee, a Ghanaian native and an ordained Anglican priest who spoke at the 1994 conference, pointed beyond those motives and toward a vision that both can protect religious human rights and can renew the mission work of religious groups: "Religion of one type or other is a living spring of life of *homo africanus* and therefore has a special place in the nurture and fostering of human rights in Africa, religious or otherwise. ... Since the two most populous religions of Africa, namely Christianity and Islam, are missionary religions, the quest for religious human rights must also search for models of mission which, from start to finish, respect and foster human dignity."

PUSHING THE FAITH: WHOSE RITES GET RIGHTS?

As the millennium became less a distant destination and more a discernible milestone, the landscape of religious rights seemed to glisten with hope.

> New global freedoms have led to clashes involving old religious rivals and new proselytizers, said John Witte, director of Emory University's law and religion program. "It is one of the bitter fruits of the religious liberty revolution around the world," he said.
>
> *The Washington Times*
> June 14, 1998

New democracies. In the final third of the 20th century, more than 30 had been born around the world.

Newly stated religious rights. More than 150 major new documents—national, regional, and international—spelled out generous protections and entitlements for religious persons and groups.

Resurging faiths. Within regions newly committed to democracy and human rights, ancient faiths once driven underground by oppressors had sprung forth with new vigor: Buddhist, Christian, Hindu, Jewish, Muslim, and an exotic array of goddess and naturalist cults.

A religious awakening. The branches of Christianity were sprouting numerous new Evangelical and Pentecostal movements. In many parts of the world, a host of new or newly minted faiths had arisen as well, including Adventists, Bahai's, Hare Krishnas, Jehovah's Witnesses, Mormons, Scientologists, and the Unification Church.

Was the world entering, then, a fresh age of religious freedom and ecumenical spirit? The law and religion scholars at Emory, who had been watching these global developments for some time, might have answered, *Not exactly.* Those most hopeful might have added, *Not yet.*

A WAR OF SOULS

As the leaders of the Center were well aware, the political transformations in parts of Russia, Eastern Europe, Africa, and Latin America had opened some long-closed doors—through which foreign religious groups were now surging. In the 1980s and

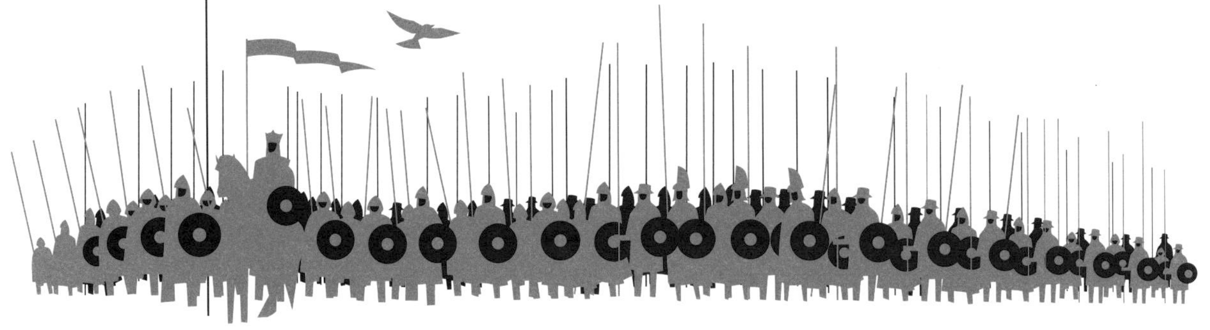

1990s, granted the right to enter these regions for the first time in decades, believers from many faiths came in increasing numbers. They were often part of well-organized and well-financed programs, to preach, to offer their services, and to convert new souls.

Even very good intentions, however, can go awry. Initially, local religious groups—Orthodox, Catholic, Protestant, Sunni, Shi'ite, and Traditional—welcomed these foreigners. Over time, the welcome waned as local religious groups began to resent some of the Western-style baggage accompanying the message of faith: materialism, individualism, and extravagant forms of religious speech, press, and assembly.

The newborn hope for a Golden Age tottered as conflict broke out in several new "democracies." In the ensuing drama, votaries and volunteers alike played the roles of victim and villain, each side demonizing the other. Taking the lead in closely studying this controversy, the Center launched a new project: "The Problem and Promise of Proselytism in the New Democratic World Order," under the leadership of John Witte, Abdullahi An-Na'im, and Johan van der Vyver. The project aimed to analyze and reconcile the "new war for souls" that proselytizing had engendered, particularly in sub-Saharan Africa, Latin America, and the former Soviet bloc.

The theaters of the new "war" were both theological and legal. Opposition propelled rival religious communities into ever more dogmatic and fundamentalist stands. Meanwhile, religious groups, seeing their indigenous faiths threatened by foreign proselytizing, began to conspire with local political leaders to adopt regulations restricting their religious rivals' constitutional rights. Several countries passed firm new anti-proselytism laws, cult registration requirements, tighter visa controls, and discriminatory restrictions on new or newly arrived religions.

Throughout the world, proselytism—spurred by motives ranging from sincere to sanctimonious, from spiritually mandated to spiritually manipulative—raised hard questions not only about rights, but also about wrongs.

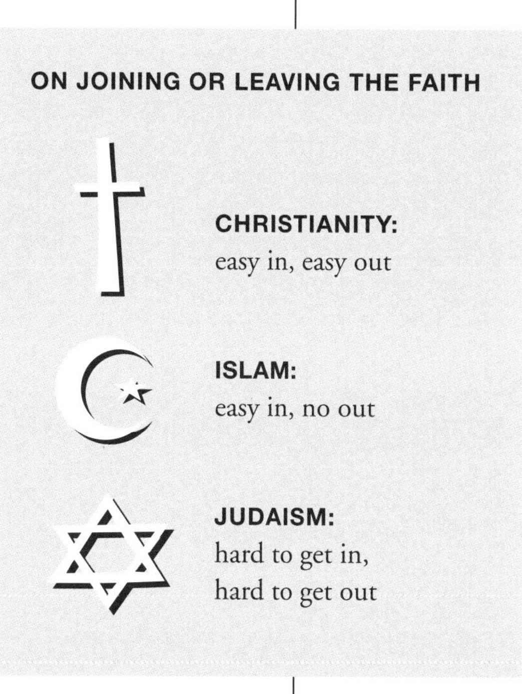

THE UNIVERSAL DECLARATION OF HUMAN RIGHTS, 1948

"Everyone has the right to freedom of thought, conscience, and religion; this right includes freedom to change his religion or belief."

THE INTERNATIONAL COVENANT ON CIVIL AND POLITICAL RIGHTS, 1966

"... This right shall include freedom to have or to adopt a religion or belief of his choice."

How does the state balance one community's right to expand its faith versus another person's or community's right to be left alone?

How does the state protect the juxtaposed rights claims of majority and minority religions, or of foreign and indigenous religions?

How does the state craft a general rule to govern multiple theological understandings of conversion or change of religion?

The Kenyan indigenous population has been subjected ... to a great deal of pressure to decide for Jesus, Allah, and lately, Asian deities. ... The most affected institution of society is the family, notably the youth.

Hannah W. Kinoti
University of Nairobi
Proselytization and Communal Self-Determination in Africa

With such questions in mind, the Center's law and religion scholars took a comprehensive look at the problem of religious proselytizing in selected parts of the world. They aimed to assess the problem through research as well as interviews and conferences on site in the most contested areas. They also sought, where possible, to seek human rights solutions that might assuage the most acute forms of conflict.

WIDENING PERSPECTIVES

The project sorted itself into regional investigations: *Russia,* Michael Bourdeaux and John Witte; *Eastern Europe,* Paul Mojzes and John Witte; *Ukraine,* Cole Durham and David Little; *Africa,* Johan van der Vyver and Abdullahi An-Na'im; *Latin America,* Paul E. Sigmund. Two additional teams took on the comparative analysis of evangelism and proselytism: *Religious Perspectives,* John Witte and Richard C. Martin; and *Legal Perspectives,* Johan van der Vyver and Abdullahi An-Na'im.

To many proponents of religion [in Eastern Europe] it seemed as if the soul of their respective nation had been either driven out or driven into the deepest recesses of the nation's collective consciousness.

Paul Mojzes, Rosemont College
Journal of Ecumenical Studies
Winter-Spring 1999

The subject's disparate immediacy lent itself not to a grand conference of hundreds, but to smaller, more intensive inquiries and conversations on site. From 1995 to 1997, the regional teams met in Atlanta, Oxford, Dresden, Princeton, Mexico City, Budapest, Dakar, Cape Town, and Moscow.

Abdullahi An-Na'im noted the freshness of this convergence: "What has been surprising is the number of scholars already doing cutting-edge research on issues related to proselytizing. This is the first time they have come together to share their work."

Ultimately, more than 160 scholars, religious leaders, and activists from around the world participated in the project, which ran until the year 2000 and produced a wealth of resources on the clashes between indigenous religions and the foreign missionizing religions seeking to compete with them.

INTERNATIONAL IMPACT

Center scholars presented results of their work at the National Press Club in June 1998, and numerous news articles followed, focusing public awareness on the global issue of proselytizing.

Increased attention to the Russian proselytizing issue helped establish the Emory law and religion scholars as experts. Having spent the past two years studying and discussing the situation, project researchers found themselves unexpectedly pressed into diplomatic or scholarly service. Project participants consulted with the U.S. State Department, Office of Security and Cooperation in Europe (OSCE), and various non-governmental organizations involved in human rights questions. They advised the U.S. State Department Committee on Religious Persecution, Vice President Al Gore and staff, and Senator Robert G. Lugar and staff. They also participated in a high-level diplomatic meeting about Russian legislation at The Hague with Russian, European, and American leaders in September 1997. Since that time, various religious organizations in Russia, notably the Jehovah's Witnesses, have been using the Center's resources in pressing their case for religious freedom in Russian courts and legislatures.

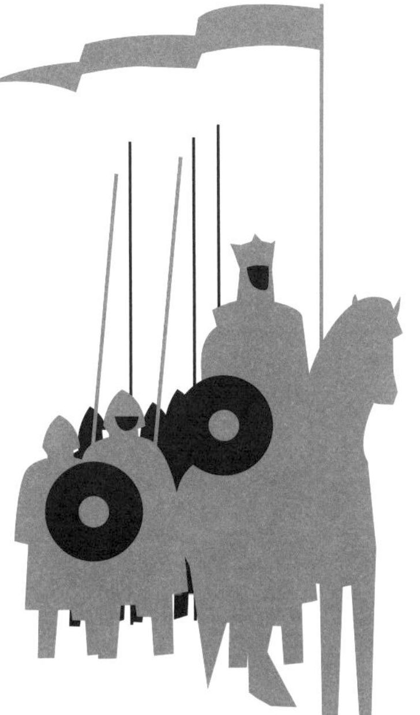

The Center's research, initiated in 1994, paved the way for other organizations. At least four new major projects soon sprang up to address this same issue—by the World Council of Churches, The Helsinki Committee, the U.S. State Department, and the OSCE.

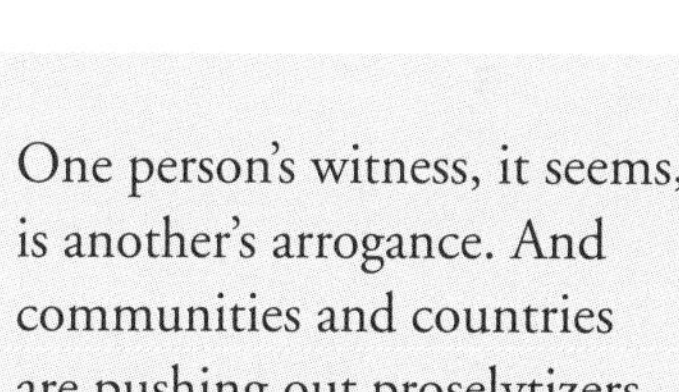

One person's witness, it seems, is another's arrogance. And communities and countries are pushing out proselytizers.

Newhouse News Service
May 30, 1998

U.S. interest in religious liberty has never been higher, as missionaries and proselytizers collide with governments and the church establishment. ... Professor John Witte, Jr., director of the law and religion program at Emory University, calls this clash '"soul wars." And it is having an impact.

Journal of Commerce
June 30, 1998

SELECTED PUBLICATIONS

The Center's teams comprehensively assessed the problem of proselytizing in selected regions.

John Witte, Jr. and Richard C. Martin, eds., *Sharing the Book: Religious Perspectives on the Rights and Wrongs of Proselytism* (Orbis Books, 1999)
An overarching perspective—covering historical and modern mission movements in Judaism, Christianity, and Islam—emerges from the 16 essays in *Sharing the Book.*

Abdullahi Ahmed An-Na'im, ed., *Proselytization and Communal Self-Determination in Africa* (Orbis Books, 1999)
In this probing collection of essays, a stellar group of Muslim and Christian, African and Western scholars explore the questions: "Where does one community's right to commend itself to others leave off, and another community's right to be left alone begin? In pluralist societies, can Islam, Christianity, and African religion coexist in peace?" Each author seeks the answers within the wider context of various African countries' complex realities: political, social, economic, ethnic, cultural, and legal.

Johan D. van der Vyver, ed., "The Problem of Proselytism in Southern Africa: Legal and Theological Dimensions," *Emory International Law Review* 14 (2000): 491-1303
The history of Southern Africa is fraught with contests among various groups over conversion and colonization, repression and revolution, proselytism and pluralism, toleration and inculturation of religions. This voluminous anthology spans the political landscape of Southern Africa via the work of 20 African scholars.

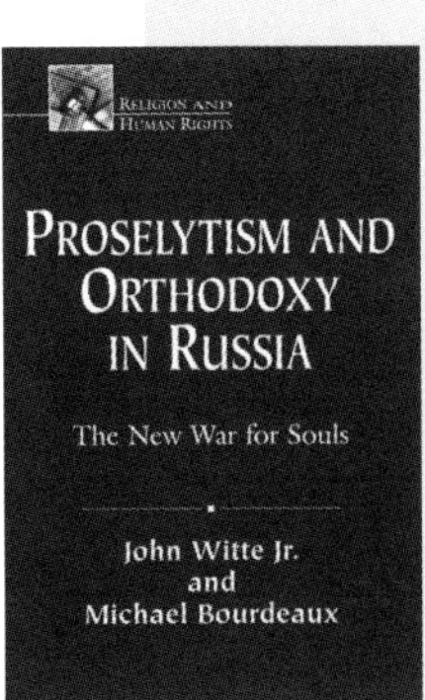

John Witte, Jr. and Michael Bourdeaux, eds., *Proselytism and Orthodoxy in Russia: The New War for Souls* (Orbis Books, 1999)
This volume assesses the legitimacy of the Orthodox Church's attempt to reclaim the spiritual and moral heart of the Russian people and to retain their adherence in a new, pluralistic world. It also brings together the latest scholarship on the new Russian laws regarding religion and suggests guidelines for foreign missionaries in Russia.

Paul E. Sigmund, ed., *Religious Freedom and Evangelization in Latin America: The Challenge of Religious Pluralism* (Orbis Books, 1999)

Symposium, "Soul Wars: The Problem of Proselytism in Russia," *Emory International Law Review* 12 (1998): 1-738

Symposium, "Pluralism, Proselytism, and Nationalism in Eastern Europe," *Journal of Ecumenical Studies* 36 (1999): 1-286

A complete listing of projects and books is available at www.law.emory.edu/cslr.

THE PROBLEM: PROMISING?

From a stance of long-perpetrated wrongs—and often a stance of "rightness"—how does one move to a position of fair and equal rights? And how does one move even beyond, to the promise of mutual respect and openness?

Article 27 of the International Covenant on Civil and Political Rights (guaranteeing religious minorities "the right ... to enjoy their own culture [and] to profess and practice their own religion") might have supported a moratorium on proselytism for a few years in places like Russia so that local religions would have had some time to recover from harsh oppression. But Article 27 cannot permanently insulate local religious groups from interaction with other religions—nor should it, because no religious and cultural tradition can remain frozen. A policy of blanket protection not only would be ultimately self-defeating, it also would stand in sharp contrast to cardinal human rights principles of openness, development, and choice.

Article 19 of the Covenant brings up another point: The right to expression, including religious expression, "carries with it special duties and responsibilities." One such duty, it would seem, is to respect the religious dignity and autonomy of the other and to expect the same respect for one's own dignity and autonomy.

This suggestion, the heart of the Golden Rule, encourages all parties, especially foreign proselytizing groups, to negotiate and adopt voluntary codes of conduct that espouse restraint and respect of others. While inter-religious dialogue and cooperation will help, they're not the only measures necessary: Every foreign mission board would do well to adopt and enforce guidelines that describe—that, in effect, promise—prudence and restraint.

Lawrence A. Uzzell, the project's Moscow representative and Director-Designate for Keston Institute, composed for *Proselytism and Orthodoxy in Russia* an essay listing 10 "Guidelines for American Missionaries in Russia," including *take the trouble to study the language, culture, and history of the people you are presuming to "save"* and *avoid behaving as if the Gospel and the American way of life are identical.*

The process of transforming such realizations into consistent practice takes focused attention. And, like the process of reviving a systematically smothered religion or of allowing a raw young democracy to mature, it takes time—the price that history invariably exacts in exchange for hope.

TRUTHS THAT MUST BE TOLD: WHOSE RESPONSIBILITY?

What is true? What is just? What is necessary?

An institution that locates its work at the convergence of law and religion must persistently consider the nature of truth, the mandates of morality, the duty of right action. Such questioning weaves in and out of all the Center's research projects, as scholars seek the slices of truth revealed through history, firsthand experience, and vigorous dialogue.

Not all of the Center's studies circle the globe. Some of the hardest work takes place in cities scattered across the United States or among Georgia's small towns; much of it happens on the Emory campus and in downtown Atlanta. Such efforts result from the particular focus of impassioned advocates —people speaking on behalf of others whose voices have been variously denied, suppressed, overlooked, or misunderstood.

Though the Center itself doesn't exist for advocacy, it fosters the work of individual scholars who fight to end social inequities and the abuses of human dignity. In the problems that these scholars investigate, the question of *Whose responsibility?* inevitably arises. The point of the question is not simply to lay blame, though guilt may surface. Rather, it asks, *Who will speak out against this wrong?* and *Who will help amend it?* At the Center, bold individual voices are bringing to public awareness a variety of injustices, challenging all of us to consider our responsibility—as citizens and as neighbors—to listen, to understand, and to help create change.

To the question *Whose responsibility?*, one answer comes from the words of Rabbi Abraham Joshua Heschel (1907-1972), who taught Jewish ethics and mysticism for almost three decades at the Jewish Theological Seminary of America and marched arm-in-arm with Martin Luther King, Jr., in Selma, Alabama. "Morally speaking, there is no limit to the concern one must feel for the suffering of human beings," he wrote in an essay from his collection *Moral Grandeur and Spiritual Audacity.* "We must continue to remind ourselves that in a free society all are involved in what some are doing. *Some are guilty, all are responsible.*"

FOR THOSE AT GROUND LEVEL: FRANK S. ALEXANDER

Law and religion. Attorney and minister. Legal systems and an unremitting care for the individual. For some, such pairings would be a difficult fence to straddle. Not for Frank Alexander, though—because he has simply removed the fence. In his life, the two seemingly disparate fields blend into a focused calling, the work he's here to do.

As an attorney poised at the exact point where law and religion intersect, he states firmly, "I want to be involved with the people who have the least. I also want to be involved with the providers of services to those people, and with the legal and political structures that *need* to be serving them."

The homeless, the down-and-out, the chronically mentally ill, the victims of credit loans, foreclosures, and evictions: these people and their suffering are never far from Alexander's awareness, even when he's in legislative overdrive. "Remembering the pain of our day-to-day lives," he says, "helps me understand the complexity that underlies each legal question. It reminds me that law can work both to liberate and to oppress."

Frank Alexander touring an Atlanta housing project, 1996

When Alexander chose to pursue graduate degrees in both law and theology (see biography, page 10), he did so with deliberate intent: Ministerial work would keep him close to the people he yearned to serve; legal study would give him the knowledge and skill to influence the law on their behalf. Today, that combination definitely works.

And so does Alexander, whose web of daily, weekly, monthly appointments would confound anyone's planner pages. Besides teaching his law classes at Emory—regularly reaching more than 200 students per year—he makes the rounds at local homeless shelters, housing projects, and housing facilities for the adult chronically mentally ill. He drafts ordinances for cities and legislation for state legislatures, testifies before legislative committees, and meets with attorneys on litigation strategies and public policy experts on development strategies. He takes a vocal role in board meetings: the Community of Friendship, Inc.; the Consumer Credit Counseling Service (CCCS); Habitat for Humanity; and the National Vacant Properties Campaign (Smart Growth Atlanta). Much of the time, he's responding to phone calls from attorneys and elected officials who want him to help brainstorm a policy, a program, or a set of laws. Journalists, too, seek his commentary for articles on topics like tax foreclosure reform and consumer law.

> Our tendency, as legal educators and students of the law, is to hide behind the words and power of the law, and this blinds us too often to the very people who are the subject of the law.
>
> **Frank S. Alexander**
> *Emory Law Journal,* 1993

And beyond all of that, he's on the road. Alexander's seminal work with land banks—public authorities that develop tax-foreclosed property in the best interests of the community—has led him into an advisory role with cities throughout the United States. For the past five years, he has traveled back and forth to Flint, Michigan, and Jacksonville, Florida, as well as to Little Rock, Indianapolis, Baltimore, and New Orleans (pre- and post-Katrina), to help these cities save their urban land. In his signature way—from the ground level up—Alexander is helping them.

FROM PROJECTS TO PUBLICATIONS

Under the broad heading **Affordable Housing and Community Development,** Alexander directs several projects that provide technical assistance to local governments and nonprofit community development organizations.

PROJECTS

Land Bank Authorities in the United States
Highlights: led legislative initiatives in Georgia and Michigan to authorize the creation of state and local land bank authorities

Technical Assistance to Local Governments on Vacant, Abandoned, and Tax Delinquent Properties
Highlights: assisted in the reform of tax foreclosure laws in Georgia, Louisiana, Michigan, Arkansas, and Indiana, and provided assistance at the local government levels to Indianapolis, Flint, Atlanta, Little Rock, Baltimore, Jacksonville, and New Orleans

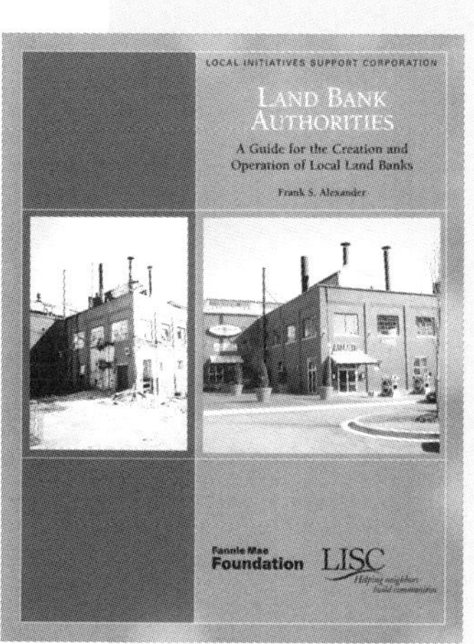

Housing & Homelessness
Highlights: served as a commissioner of the State Housing Trust Fund for the Homeless, authored a report on the creation of local government housing trust funds in Georgia

PUBLICATIONS: FRANK ALEXANDER

Land Bank Authorities: A Guide for the Creation and Operation of Local Land Banks (Fannie Mae Foundation/LISC, 2005)
A roadmap for cities and counties rediscovering the value of urban land, this guidebook chronicles the development of the nation's first land banks—in St. Louis, Cleveland, Louisville, Atlanta, and Genesee County, Michigan—describing the conditions, history, and legal structures of each.

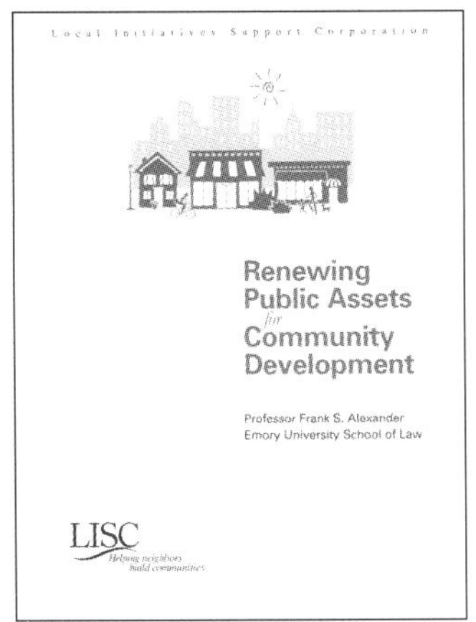

Renewing Public Assets for Community Development (Fannie Mae Foundation, 2002)
Two public assets are central to community development: delinquent tax liens and government owned land. Through this basic overview, Alexander equips community development organizations and local government officials to analyze and reform the applicable laws of their cities and counties.

"The Housing of America's Families: Control, Exclusion and Privilege," *Emory Law Journal* 54 (2005): 1231-1270

Housing Trust Funds for Local Governments in Georgia (Fannie Mae Foundation, 2002)

A City for All: Report of the Gentrification Task Force of the Atlanta City Council (Fannie Mae Foundation, 2001)

Renewing Public Assets for Community Development (LISC, 2000)

KEEPING THE TRUTH ALIVE: DEBORAH LIPSTADT

When Emory Professor Deborah Lipstadt wrote *Denying the Holocaust: The Growing Assault on Truth and Memory* (1994), she spent, by her estimate, "a couple of hundred words" on the work of British historian David Irving (*Hitler's War,* 1977), whom she called a Holocaust denier and a manipulator of evidence. In 1996, shortly after the book's publication in the United Kingdom, Irving sued both Lipstadt and Penguin UK for libel. The sensational nine-week trial in the English High Court, widely covered by the media, ended on April 11, 2000, when Justice Charles Gray delivered a 333-page decision assessing Irving not only as a racist and anti-Semitic Holocaust denier, but also as a liar.

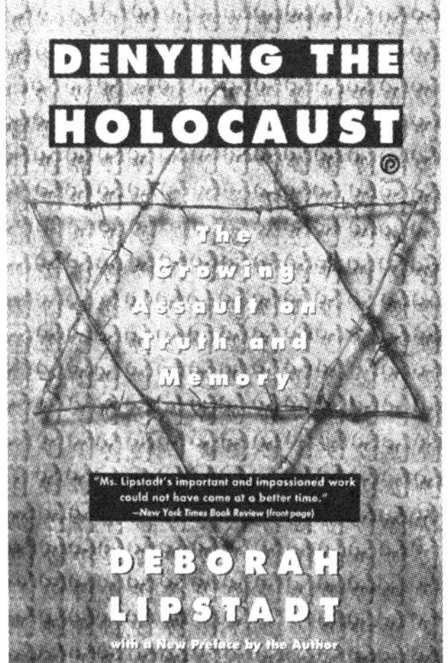

After the verdict, Lipstadt said she had challenged Irving because "the truth has to be kept alive."

"As [Holocaust] survivors die off and there are fewer and fewer eyewitnesses, there won't be people to tell the story in the first person, and it will be easier to deny it." (*Washington Post,* April 12, 2000.)

Numerous editorials hailed the judgment. *The New York Times* declared that the verdict put an end to the pretense that Mr. Irving is anything but "a self-promoting apologist for Hitler." (April 14, 2000). *The London Times* said that "history has had its day in court and scored a crushing victory." (April 12, 2000).

CSLR hosted two conferences on the Lipstadt trial as part of the Center's ongoing project on Jewish Legal Studies. Directed by CSLR Senior Fellows Michael J. Broyde and Michael S. Berger, Emory Associate Professor of Religion, "Irving v. Penguin Books and Deborah Lipstadt" (2000-2001) celebrated Lipstadt's successful defense, capped the history-making experience, and began serious reflection on its implications.

The first conference, in September 2000, drew 1,000 people. The evening program on "Holocaust Denial: Theological Reflections" featured lectures by Lipstadt and Rabbi Dr. Norman Lamm, president of Yeshiva University and a former teacher of Lipstadts.

November of that year brought another full house for the second conference, titled "Reconciling the Irreconcilable?: Holocaust Denial, Historical Truth, and Jewish Identity." The keynote speaker was Richard Rampton, Q.C., who had successfully defended Lipstadt and Penguin Books against David Irving's libel claim. Sessions explored the intellectual issues surrounding Holocaust denial, from international law to American tort law, contemporary Israeli responses to the phenomenon, free speech at the academy, and a First Amendment perspective. Speakers included Lipstadt; Shalom Goldman, Emory professor of Hebrew and Middle Eastern Studies; and Anita Bernstein and David Bederman, both Emory law professors. Stanley Fish, then dean of the College of Liberal Arts and Sciences at the University of Illinois at Chicago, also lectured.

The trial and the conferences were landmark events in the emerging big conversations on human rights and on legal issues related to Judaism. Lipstadt, an associated faculty member at the Center, continues her multiple roles of teaching, writing, advising, and counseling—all in the service of fighting attempts to pervert, distort, and lie about history.

Deborah E. Lipstadt
Ph.D., Brandeis University
Dorot Professor of Modern Jewish and Holocaust Studies, Emory University
Director, Rabbi A. Tam Institute for Jewish Studies
CSLR Associated Faculty

Deborah Lipstadt has received multiple awards for her teaching at Emory. Owing to her expertise, she has received numerous advisory positions. In recent years Lipstadt has served as a historical consultant to the United States Holocaust Memorial Museum; as a member of the United States Holocaust Memorial Council; and as a member of the United States State Department Advisory Committee on Religious Freedom. Lipstadt's frequent appearances and commentary in the national and international media have made her name almost a household word, standing both for scholarship and for service. The Jewish Council for Public Affairs honored Lipstadt with the Al Chernin Award, given to the person who best exemplifies protection of the First Amendment.

FAMILIES MATTER: FRANCES SMITH FOSTER

Frances Foster's study of early African American families, as part of the Center's project "Sex, Marriage, and Family & the Religions of the Book," also seeks the truth.

African American families have too long been represented as pitiful, Foster declares in her study *Families Matter: Representations of Family and Marriage in the Antebellum Afro-Protestant Press.* "Usually when people talk about matters such as family or marriage, especially among antebellum African Americans, they focus upon fractures and fissures, victims and fugitives ... [the] progeny and progenitors of dysfunctional, unstable and even unnatural families."

That impression contains some truth; certainly, slavery and racism took their toll on the health of black and white families alike. But Foster has asked some essential questions—*Whose stories have we ignored? Whose voices have we not heard?*—and her years of research have provided answers that balance popular conceptions of beleaguered black families with both fictional and nonfictional accounts in which family members love each other, help each other, and persist despite adverse conditions.

Furthermore, as Foster's essay points out, in antebellum society, "*African American* is not a synonym for *slave* ... From the earliest arrivals in North America, some Africans and people of African descent were at least as free, educated, and as financially solvent as Euro-American indentured servants or working-class Americans. In the antebellum period, census figures record nearly a half million free African Americans."

From eye-straining microfilm and age-brittled handwritten documents to modern reproductions and online archives, Foster has examined a wealth of 18th- and 19th-century sources. Among these are Emory's special collection on the free black press that includes the complete run of *Freedom's Journal*—the first African American owned and operated newspaper in the United States, published weekly in New York City from 1827 to 1829 and circulated in 11 states, the District of Columbia, Haiti, Europe, and Canada. A key discovery in Foster's research is the extent to which Afro-Protestant churches enabled communication among African Americans. They printed and distributed newspapers, magazines, pamphlets, and separately published volumes in an effort collectively called the Afro-Protestant Press. The result of her work is three new volumes: *Love and Marriage in Early African America; "'Til Death – or Distance Do Us Part": Love, Marriage and Gender Matters in Antebellum African America;* and *Family in Africa and the African Diaspora: A Multidisciplinary Approach.*

In *Family in Africa and the African Diaspora,* Foster writes, "Though attacked and wounded, fractured and dispersed, not all African American families were destroyed nor all bloodlines broken. Indeed many of the writings in the Afro-Protestant Press may be interpreted as demonstrating that even when deliberately unraveled, African American families re-knit themselves into kinship communities of families ... that in fact functioned effectively enough to teach self-esteem and to encourage resistance to enslavement, to offer some physical protection and practical advice, and to preserve and perpetuate cultural practices."

By ensuring that some long-buried stories are now being told, Foster, in her unique way, is bringing to light a more truthful perspective on a painful subject.

Frances Smith Foster
Ph.D., University of California, San Diego
Charles Howard Candler Professor of English and Women's Studies,
Emory University
CSLR Senior Fellow

An enthusiastic mother and grandmother as well as scholar, Foster has established a compatible and compelling niche for her research: family life and personal narratives among early African Americans. It's a broadening niche for her students in literature and women's studies, who sample Foster's research in courses such as "Slavery and the African American Literary Imagination," "Writing Things Right in Nineteenth Century African American Literature," and "Family, Marriage, and Sexual Morality in Early African America." She is the author of *Written by Herself: Literary Production by African American Women, 1726-1892,* and an editor of the *Oxford Companion to African American Literature*; *The Norton Anthology of African American Literature,* and *Incidents in the Life of a Slave Girl: A Norton Critical Edition.*

PUBLICATIONS: FRANCES FOSTER

Love and Marriage in Early African America
(Northeastern University Press, 2007)
This volume brings together a remarkable range of folk sayings, songs, poems, letters, lectures, sermons, short stories, memoirs, and autobiographies, many of which are previously unknown or difficult to access. Spanning over 100 years, from the slave era to the New Negro Movement, the collection also alters our ideas about the relationship between religion and politics in early African America.

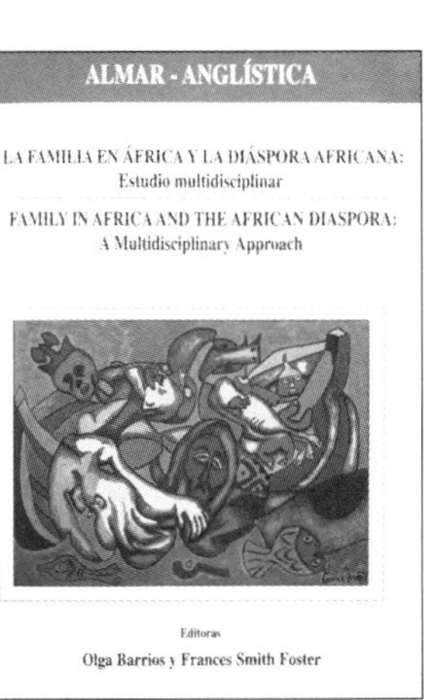

Family in Africa and the African Diaspora: A Multidisciplinary Approach
(Salamanca: Almar-Anglistica, 2004)
A bilingual anthology, this book gathers essays focused on such topics as family and society, family in the visual and performing arts, and family in literature, by scholars and artists from Canada, Ethiopia, Ghana, Jamaica, South Africa, Spain, and the United States. The collection contains Foster's essay "Families Matter: Representations of Family and Marriage in the Antebellum Afro-Protestant Press," as well as illustrations by Tomás González Pérez and an introduction by poet Velma Pollard.

FOR THOSE MOST VULNERABLE: KAREN WORTHINGTON

Fact: Each year, nearly a million U.S. children are abused or neglected.
Fact: On any given day, between 16,000 and 18,000 of those children are in the legal custody of the State of Georgia.

These two facts continually sharpen the zeal of Karen Worthington, who states unequivocally, "I'm a strident child advocate." Founding director of the Barton Child Law and Policy Clinic, housed in Emory Law School, Worthington adds, "All of my work aims to influence public policy and improve the lives of children in foster care. They are Georgia's most vulnerable residents."

She maintains her single-minded focus through a whirlwind of administrative and advocacy activities. Since its founding in 2000, the Barton Clinic has helped Georgia serve neglected and abused children by providing multidisciplinary, child-focused research, training, and support for practitioners and policy-makers charged with protecting these vulnerable ones. Much more than an advocacy group, the Clinic supervises more than 30 students each year—from disciplines such as law, social work, public health, and theology—who work in Georgia's child welfare system. Barton Clinic's programs also train hundreds of professionals in Georgia and across the country; its post-graduate fellowship in law attracts applicants from the top schools in the nation.

Worthington's work takes her from computer to classroom, from legislative settings to the lecturn—and back again—as she writes white papers, policy documents, and drafts of legislative amendments; teaches, supervises, and mentors the Clinic's students; testifies before legislative committees and meets with policy-makers. And that short list barely scratches the surface—omitting her ongoing work with fundraising, research, and public presentations.

Worthington published *Georgia's Responsibilities Toward Children in Foster Care: A Reference Manual* in 2005. This long-needed compendium brought all sources together in one volume—while clearing away some accumulated bureaucratic debris. The manual is for everyone involved in Georgia's child welfare system—elected officials, case workers, foster parents, and the children themselves. Worthington's theory: Once people know exactly what the state is responsible for, they can begin to make sure that the state comes through.

Karen Worthington
J.D., Emory University
Founding Director, Barton Child Law and Policy Clinic
CSLR Senior Fellow

Karen Worthington—professor, administrator, advocate—came to Emory in March 2000 as director of the newly created Barton Child Law and Policy Clinic. In addition to directing the Clinic's activities, supervising its students, and teaching child advocacy, she also supervises the Emory Summer Child Advocacy Program and the Clinic's juvenile defender service. Worthington works to improve the treatment of children in state custody by improving the systems responsible for caring for those children. She specializes in both child welfare and juvenile delinquency concerns and is a frequent presenter and facilitator at conferences and training sessions throughout Georgia and beyond.

PUBLICATIONS: KAREN WORTHINGTON

Georgia's Responsibilities Toward Children in Foster Care: A Reference Manual (Barton Child Law and Policy Clinic, 2005)

What is Right for Children? Competing Paradigms of Religion and Human Rights (with Martha A. Fineman) (forthcoming)

Representing the Whole Child: A Juvenile Defender Training Manual (Southern Juvenile Defender Center of Emory University, 2005)

BEYOND "AMEN" TO ACTION: ROBERT M. FRANKLIN

Amen. From its Hebrew origins, the word suggests *certainty.* It's a variant on the Hebrew word for *truth,* notes Robert M. Franklin. Familiarly used in the rhythmic "call and response" pattern of black church culture, "Amen" ratifies, seals, and adds the stamp of approval. After the acknowledged truth of "Amen," what could possibly follow?

Franklin answers in one word: *Action.*

Since 2004, when comedian Bill Cosby began urging increased personal and parental responsibility as a way for African Americans in poverty to hoist themselves and their children to a better life, Franklin has been shaping a campaign of his own. In February 2005, he laid out its structure to a full house during a lecture through the Center's Family Forum Series, and his new book fills in the rest of the details. Titled *Crisis in the Village: Restoring Hope in African American Communities,* the book is a call to frank conversation and then—once the "Amen" has resounded—to action marked by commitment and focus.

Two good ways to begin, Franklin advised in his lecture, "Cosby's Call and Our Response: What the Church and Community Should Do," involve reducing the country's prison population and promoting healthy marriages. "To jump start this work," he said, "we need to begin a village-wide conversation about the future of the village and especially the bedrock institution of the family. Not just in the black community, but in all of our villages."

To move toward measurable solutions for the problems of poor communities, the village-wide conversation needs to include incisive questions such as these:

What do we expect from every father and mother in the community?

What can we guarantee to all of the children in our communities?

What things do people who are considering divorce need to think about?

Where can people who are being abused in relationships turn for help?

What should each congregation in this zip code be doing to provide safe space in the after-school hours?

And because the village must go far past the "Amen," another question must follow: *By what date will we expect to see significant, measurable change?*

Franklin's work and public presence cast him in a potent combination of roles: Guardian. Advocate. Prophet. Introducing him at a recent event, John Witte called him "one of the intellectual treasures of the Emory University campus." So Franklin has had some high expectations to live up to—but he's had plenty of practice, thanks to what he describes as "an extraordinary extended family network" of encouragers in his boyhood years. And he has set for himself another guideline as well. *Crisis in the Village* emphasizes a quality essential to leaders—and similarly essential to guardians, advocates, and prophets: "Leaders who are unaware of, or uncomfortable with engaging and addressing, *the pain of the people* are unlikely to mobilize *the power of the people.*"

Concluding his response to Bill Cosby, Franklin told his audience, "I hope you will find this proposal worthy of more than a casual 'Amen, brother.'" But the call to America's villages must not discount the value of that initial "Amen," for this one affirming impulse, whether spoken or tacit, brings the glimpse of truth on which all life-changing action depends.

Robert M. Franklin
Ph.D., University of Chicago
President, Morehouse College
CSLR Senior Fellow

Robert Franklin's most recent honor settled around his shoulders when he was selected as the 10th president of his undergraduate alma mater, Morehouse College. Long before that, however, he enjoyed the honor of serving in many other key roles. He was president of the Interdenominational Theological Center; a visiting professor at the Harvard Divinity School; dean of Black Church Studies at Colgate Rochester Divinity School; director of Black Church Studies at Emory; a program officer in Human Rights and Social Justice at the Ford Foundation; and a Theologian in Residence for the Chautauqua Institution. In another influential role, Franklin is a frequent commentator for National Public Radio's "All Things Considered." Besides *Crisis in the Village,* his books include *Liberating Visions: Human Fulfillment and Social Justice in African American Thought* and *Another Day's Journey: Black Churches Confronting the American Crisis.* With CSLR Visiting Professor Don S. Browning and others, he co-authored *From Culture Wars to Common Ground: Religion and the American Family Debate.*

LAW AND RELIGION, APPLIED

Frank Alexander, reflecting on his work and that of Deborah Lipstadt, Frances Foster, Karen Worthington, and Robert Franklin, said, "All of us do what I would call *law and religion, applied.* As five very different examples of individuals sharing convictions about the relevancy of ministry to the law, we help illustrate some of the rich possibilities within that convergence."

As these five scholars—and many others like them—continue to ask, *What is true? What is just? What is necessary?,* another bit of folk wisdom, cited by Franklin in *Crisis in the Village,* bears repeating.

Franklin recalls, "I didn't want to write this book. I was waiting for someone else to do it." During that period of waiting and reluctance, he heard two different people cite an admonition that he found uncannily pertinent—and that compelled him to action.

Marian Wright Edelman quoted Mahatma Gandhi: "We must be the change that we seek."

Jim Wallis of *Sojourners* magazine quoted the young African organizer Lisa Sullivan: "We are the ones we've been waiting for."

MODERN ISLAM: CAN CONSTITUTIONALISM THRIVE?

"I quote Gandhi all the time: *Be the change you want to make.* Taha, my own teacher in Sudan, used to say the same. For 18 years I was with him, ever since I was a law student in the '60s. His point was that we must accept responsibility for our lives, and keep consistency between our thought, speech, and action."

Abdullahi An-Na'im has kept that consistency and will continue to keep it.

In the more than 20 years since his mentor Mahmoud Muhammad Taha was executed for heresy, An-Na'im has endeavored to honor the teachings of Taha, who opposed basing the constitution of Sudan on a strict interpretation of Shari'a, or Islamic law. Taha held that Shari'a needed reforming, that the ancient sacred texts of Islam themselves support such change.

Like Taha, An-Na'im is a devout Muslim and a political dissident; unlike Taha, he's a jurist—and an exile. An-Na'im fled Sudan in 1985, creating a path that led finally to Emory's Center for the Study of Law and Religion, which he joined in 1995 (see biography, page 23). At the Center, he has found what he calls "a home, intellectual and human," along with the environment and support that propel his life's work: helping the world's 1.3 billion Muslims recognize—and act on—the possibilities that exist within their faith, their countries' governments, and their individual lives.

I am a Muslim, but I couldn't accept Shari'a ... I couldn't see how Sudan could be viable without women being full citizens and without non-Muslims being full citizens.

Abdullahi Ahmed An-Na'im
The New Yorker
September 11, 2006

PRICE $3.99 THE SEPT. 11, 2006
NEW YORKER

LETTER FROM SUDAN

THE MODERATE MARTYR

A radically peaceful vision of Islam.

BY GEORGE PACKER

Courtesy of *The New Yorker*/ Condé Nast Publications Inc; Guy Billout (illustration); John Mavroudis and Owen Smith ("Soaring Spirit" cover)

THE LANDSCAPE OF HUMAN RIGHTS

An-Na'im has directed several projects, all with a long and deep reach. Some of his initial research involved cultural transformation and human rights in Africa, followed by a global survey of the most widely applied family law system in the world today: Islamic family law. From the outset, An-Na'im viewed his work through the lens of human rights, especially the rights of women and children, and as an essential first step in a methodical progression of research, analysis, law reform proposals, and active advocacy for change.

"It is not good enough," wrote An-Na'im in *Islam and Human Rights: Advocacy for Social Change in Local Contexts*, "to have the best ideas and arguments for public policy, without the effective ability to communicate and translate them into practical strategies for social transformation."

Under An-Na'im's direction, the Human Rights Fellowship Program, a four-year project at the Center funded by the Ford Foundation, brought together 10 resident scholars and activists from the Islamic world to study the relationship between human rights and Islam. The team's study went worldwide and yielded the *Islam and Human Rights* volume. It also prompted what has become An-Na'im's signature: interactive websites, designed to invite the widest possible participation by opening the door to intellectual exchange, debate, and shared resources, thus establishing a permanent network of people working in this field. The scholarly momentum continued, as his study of Africa's incremental constitutionalism produced *African Constitutionalism and the Role of Islam*.

THE FUTURE OF SHARI'A

How can Muslims influence the intricate and volatile relationship of religion and law in the double context of modern Islam and the modern world?

Given Islam's connection with politics, how can a separation of religion and state in predominantly Islamic countries actually work?

How can a modernized Shari'a foster human rights?

How can a secular state, in fact, help believers be better Muslims?

For a long time, An-Na'im has asked himself such questions. Through his research project "The Future of Shari'a in Islamic Societies," with its 10 international seminars and its interactive website, he has asked colleagues and fellow Muslims worldwide. The results have now begun to go global—and in a range of native languages: Indonesian, Arabic, Bengali, Persian, Russian, Turkish, French, and Urdu.

An-Na'im's legacy book *Islam and the Secular State: Negotiating the Future of Shari'a*, written from a compassionate insider's point of view, analyzes the relationship of religion, state, and society in its specifically Islamic context, paying particular attention to the ongoing interpretation of ancient texts and the post-colonial condition of Islamic countries. Chapters in eight languages are posted online (www.law.emory.edu/FS/), to invite international dialogue. The full book was originally published in Indonesian in 2007.

Abdullahi An-Na'im on book tour in Indonesia, 2007

Summer 2007 took An-Na'im on the initial book-launch trip—to Indonesia, specially selected for the study's first published version because the vast majority of Indonesian Muslims are already committed to a secular state. The intense four-week tour—a whirlwind of presentations as well as interviews with magazines, newspapers, and radio—generated op-ed pieces and even a cover issue of a populist Islamic magazine. This positive reception, said An-Na'im, "was exactly what I was hoping for."

"Shari'a *has* a future; there's no doubt in my mind about that," said An-Na'im in a January 2007 lecture at Emory. "My whole object is to fulfill, secure, and promote its future. But that future can only be outside the state. Muslims are bound to observe Shari'a, no matter what the state does or fails to do. We can never do so, however, except by choice. Any coercion is not religious—it causes Shari'a to lose the quality of being Islamic. Shari'a is too important to be entrusted to the state."

THE CASE FOR A SECULAR STATE

Over decades of study, An-Na'im has substantially worked with Taha's views to develop an argument for a secular state. His appeal to Muslims reflects both the logic of a legal scholar and the candor of a kinsman:

- Though Shari'a is often called Islamic law, it's more accurately defined as a religious normative system. It's the door and passageway into being Muslim.
- For every individual Muslim, according to the Qur'an, knowing and upholding Shari'a is a responsibility that is inescapable, that cannot be delegated.
- As soon as a state enacts a law based on the system of Shari'a, two things automatically result: Shari'a loses its religious nature, and the state usurps the individual Muslim's right to fulfill his or her religious responsibility.
- Because the state is a political institution, it cannot simultaneously be religious.

Therefore, a so-called "Islamic state" can't actually exist.

- The most viable alternative, called the "secular state," is different from its popular conception. A state that acknowledges its secular role is actually leaving religion to the care of the people, which is exactly where religion belongs.

- A secular state promotes honest piety rather than hypocrisy; it acts as a guardian of human rights; and by not obstructing the possibility of dissent, it helps keep faith alive and vital.

- Although public gaze is currently riveted on the conflicts in the Middle East, those events do not represent the reality of most Muslim societies today. In fact, the majority of the world's Muslims already live in secular states and are comfortable with that condition. They don't see having a secular state as inconsistent with being Muslim.

Therefore, a secular state is not by definition anti-religious.

- Post-colonial societies (including every Muslim country today), being relatively new to self-governance, still have much to learn—either from the time-consuming trial and error of their own mistakes, or from the mistakes of others.

- Change in a society, to be sustainable, cannot emerge through external imposition but must be interwoven with the everyday lives and social practices of the people.

- The proponents of change must not only have a credible claim to being insiders in the culture, but also must use valid arguments to persuade the local population.

Therefore, Islamic reform should not, indeed cannot, come through a wholesale, uncritical adoption of dominant Western theories and practices.

- There is no easy, formulaic solution to the paradox of separating Islam and the state while at the same time regulating an organic relationship among Islam, state, and politics.

- This mediation of paradox should be based on distinction between the institutional continuity of the state, on one hand, and the contingencies of politics, which is reflected in the government of the day that can change through the democratic process.

- Only proactive social interaction—reasoned public discourse, practiced over time—can help navigate this paradox.

> In the final analysis, the question is how to communicate and link the rationality of constitutional ideals with the economic, social, or contextual realities of the people concerned.
>
> **Abdullahi Ahmed An-Na'im**
> *African Constitutionalism and the Role of Islam*

> A human rights theory is good only to the extent that it can be translated into practice to improve the daily lives of people.
>
> An-Na'im, from the "Islam and Human Rights" website

ONLINE SCHOLARSHIP, DIALOGUE, AND ADVOCACY

An-Na'im uses websites to spark international dialogue about his research.

The Future of Shari'a: www.law.emory.edu/FS/
Languages: Arabic, Bahasa, Bengali, English, French, Persian, Russian, Turkish, Urdu. Visitors to this site can download and comment on draft chapters from An-Na'im's 2007 book, *Islam and the Secular State: Negotiating the Future of Shari'a,* and view a webcast of his Center lecture on this topic.

Islam and Human Rights: www.law.emory.edu/IHR
Languages: Bahasa, English, French, Persian, Urdu. The user-friendly site includes "Voices from Participants" (dialogue and discussion); accessibly indexed scholar profiles; contact information; links to other electronic resources; and recorded presentations from the International Conference in Istanbul.

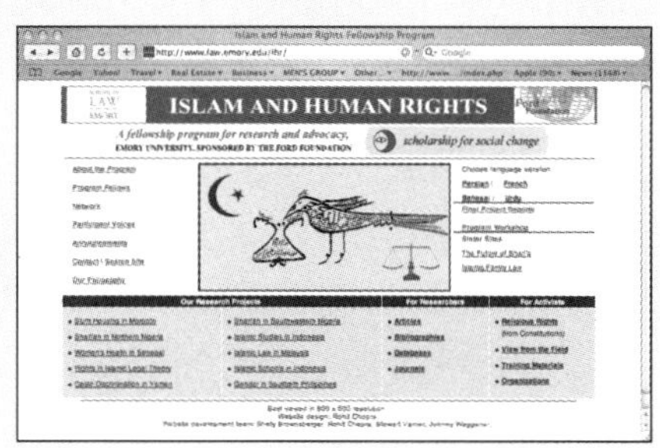

Islamic Family Law: www.law.emory.edu/IFL/
The site features a bulletin board as well as a global survey that delivers social/cultural information by geographic region; legal profiles by country; case studies; and contact information.

Women and Land in Africa: www.law.emory.edu/wandl/
The site features results of studies on woman and land ownership in seven countries; an advocacy model for how to own land; and listings of relevant literature and websites.

FROM PROJECTS TO PUBLICATIONS

Under the broad project title "Islamic Legal Studies," An-Na'im has directed explorations of the fraught relationship between Islam and Shari'a, as well as law, human rights, constitutionalism, and secularism in different parts of the world.

PROJECTS

Islamic Family Law Project (1998 - 2005)
A comprehensive analysis of the sources and scope of Islamic family law around the world, and of possible reforms in international and domestic human rights.
Highlights: three books

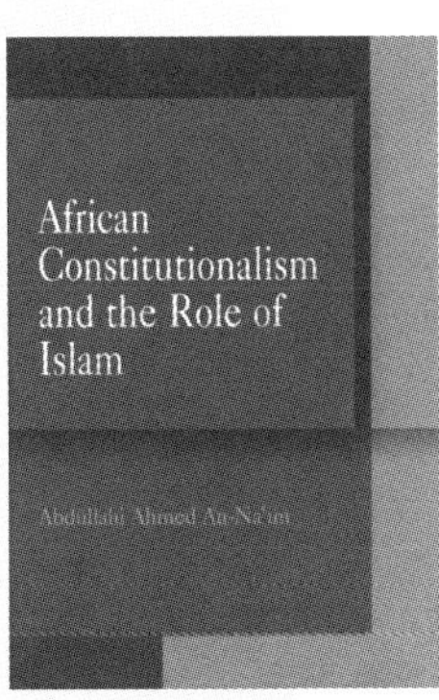

Islam and Human Rights Fellowship Program (2001 - 2005)
A residential program for scholars and activists from various parts of the Islamic world, who teamed up to examine and describe the relationship between human rights and Islam.
Highlights: 12 roundtable conferences, International Conference in Istanbul, 29 international lectures, 38 national lectures, journal symposium and special journal issue

The Future of Shari'a in Islamic Societies (2004 - 2006)
A wide-ranging study of the Islamic argument for secularism and against the idea of an Islamic state, through seminars and workshops in various countries and a published volume.
Highlights: a book (being published in numerous languages), 10 seminars and workshops in Egypt, Indonesia, Sudan, and Turkey

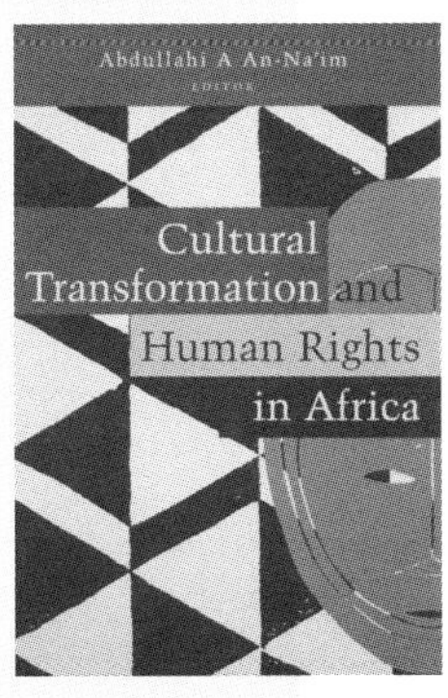

PUBLICATIONS

Abdullahi Ahmed An-Na'im, *Islam and the Secular State: Negotiating the Future of Shari'a* (Harvard University Press, 2008)

Abdullahi Ahmed An-Na'im, *African Constitutionalism and the Role of Islam* (University of Pennsylvania Press, 2006)

Abdullahi Ahmed An-Na'im, *Cultural Transformation and Human Rights in Africa* (Zed Books, 2002)

Abdullahi Ahmed An-Na'im, ed., *Islamic Family Law in a Changing World: A Global Resource Book* (Zed Books, 2002)

Mashood Baderin, Mahmood Monshipouri, Lynn Welchman, and Shadi Mokhtari, eds., *Islam and Human Rights: Advocacy for Social Change in Local Contexts* (Global Media, 2006); foreword by Abdullahi Ahmed An-Na'im

Lynn Welchman, ed. *Women's Rights and Islamic Family Law: Perspectives on Reform* (Zed Books, 2004); series editor Abdullahi Ahmed An-Na'im

FOR BETTER, FOR WORSE: BY WHOSE DECREE?

An intimate relationship, a marriage, the family circle: According to tradition, they all belong together within the lifelong joining of one man and one woman—"for better, for worse," says the standard Christian wedding vow.

But tradition, despite society's attempts to enforce, idealize, and even sanctify it, undergoes continual jostling by time and by simple human nature. Thus sexual relationships may displace or dissolve a marriage; a marriage may not expand into a family; a family group may lack wedded parents.

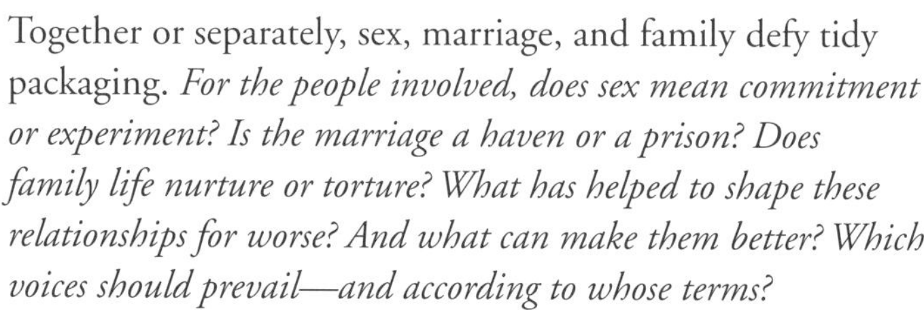

Together or separately, sex, marriage, and family defy tidy packaging. *For the people involved, does sex mean commitment or experiment? Is the marriage a haven or a prison? Does family life nurture or torture? What has helped to shape these relationships for worse? And what can make them better? Which voices should prevail—and according to whose terms?*

When the Center began work on the project "Sex, Marriage, and Family & the Religions of the Book," questions branched and rebranched at a dizzying pace. Regarding the sexual relationships, marriages, and families of today, almost every possible inquiry exists. *Who, what, when, where, why,* and *how* are only the beginning. Each one of those inquiries must raise its negative as well: *Who's legally married, and who isn't? Who's accountable for the children; who's not accountable? Who gets the property, and who doesn't?* The questions often hinge on a tacit, pre-established understanding of *should.*

Many time-honored traditions of sex, marriage, and family have now become time-worn. In light of changing conditions, every facet of these topics requires re-evaluation: *What's decreed? What's anathema? What's negotiable?* And though individual voices matter, both church and state—those fundamental, inescapable institutions—must also claim their say.

STATE OF THE UNIONS

In 2001, when the Center inaugurated its Sex, Marriage, and Family project, statistics about the family were grim.

Between 1975 and 2000 in the United States:

- a quarter of all pregnancies were aborted
- one-third of all children were born to single mothers

- half of all marriages ended in divorce
- two-thirds of all juvenile offenders came from broken homes
- three-quarters of all African American children were raised without fathers in the home

Furthermore, the previous four decades had seen a doubling of divorce rates in the United Kingdom, France, and Australia. And while marriage rates had decreased dramatically, illegitimacy, domestic violence, and sexually transmitted diseases had increased around the globe.

The Center sought scholars eager to consult the data, ask the probing questions, delve into the history, invite all the voices—and, through conversation and research, to assess the damage done and the possibilities for reconstruction.

Fall 2001 brought the project's kickoff seminar, an assembly of experts from varied disciplines across the university, charged with examining issues of marriage, sex, and family in relation to the "religions of the Book"—Christianity, Judaism, and Islam. The field was wide open, welcoming explorations of interfaith marriage, American divorce laws, same-sex unions, Islamic family law, child custody, sexual identity, intergenerational relations, abortions, euthanasia, contraceptive practices, cloning, the depiction of women in the Hebrew Bible, and more.

Don Browning, who co-directed the project with John Witte and served as the Center's first Robert W. Woodruff Visiting Professor of Interdisiplinary Studies, modestly described his role in the seminar as "a glorified discussion leader." He and Witte guided the project's shape, eliciting from the participants increasingly pointed areas of focus.

As in all the Center's signature seminars, the learning traveled both ways. Browning recalls: "My book on marriage and modernization incorporated much of what I learned that year. The books I've written since then have been pulled out of me by virtue of that project's synergy and momentum." (See "From Projects to Publications," page 77.)

Browning's work demonstrates that practical theology can be applied to help families in modern society. In *Equality and the Family,* he writes, "[M]y position is pro-family and pro-marriage but in ways that will promote justice and equality … and create a society that will support what I call the equal-regard family."

By no means is marriage only religious and only private. It's also a public institution—and there are big stakes in regulating the issues that it engenders.

Don S. Browning
"Sex, Marriage, and Family & the Religions of the Book" conference address

Don S. Browning
Ph.D., University of Chicago
Alexander Campbell Professor of Ethics and the Social Sciences Emeritus, University of Chicago
Robert W. Woodruff Visiting Professor of Interdisciplinary Religious Studies, Emory University

What I bring to the table, I hope, is a respect for the different voices and the various disciplines they represent. In seeking answers to big, complex questions, a narrow view of law or social sciences or economics just isn't enough. The work requires multidimensionality—good, practical thinking that spans policy issues, moral issues, and legal issues.

"I'm an interdisciplinary addict," says Browning. That trait made him a natural match with Emory's Center for the Study of Law and Religion—as did his many years of leadership in the University of Chicago's enormously influential Religion, Culture, and Family Project, which yielded 15 new volumes, hundreds of scholarly articles, and scores of public forums and conferences. His concluding work in that role, where he raised more than $4 million in foundation grants, was *Marriage: Just a Piece of Paper?*, produced as a book and as a documentary film for national television. Browning has published 20 books during his career—eight during his six-year affiliation with the Center—focusing on cultural, theological, and ethical analysis of the modern family. At the Center, he has lent his prodigious scholarship to multiple projects: "Christian Jurisprudence"; "Moral and Religious Foundations of Law"; "Sex, Marriage, and Family & the Religions of the Book"; "The Child in Law, Religion, and Society." A new anthology published in honor of Browning, *The Equal Regard Family and its Friendly Critics: Don Browning and the Practical Theological Ethics of the Family*, co-edited by Witte, M. Christian Green, and Amy Wheeler, provides an authoritative assessment of his rich contributions to the interdisciplinary study of marriage and family life.

IN THE PUBLIC EYE

The Center's leaders and fellows, accustomed to media requests for expert viewpoints, were hardly strangers to public attention. But in early 2002—after the *Boston Globe* ran its shocking story about the Catholic Church covering up the sexual misconduct of priests—the Center's scholarship on the subject of homosexuality and the church received nationwide notice, fueled by the research of Mark D. Jordan, Asa Griggs Candler Professor of Religion at Emory.

Initially, Jordan's groundbreaking book on the subject, *The Silence of Sodom: Homosexuality in Modern Catholicism* (2001), was reputedly too "hard" to be reviewed by the news media. But during the media's coverage of the priesthood scandal, Jordan recalls hearing a new response from reporters: "I've had your book on my desk for a long time, but I could never get around to it. Now it's required reading!"

"I never could have anticipated being—for the proverbial 15 minutes—an unkempt talking head on the national news circuit. Some days I would have phone messages waiting from ABC, CNN, *The Wall Street Journal*, and *The New York Times*, and I'd be trying to decide which one I should take first," said Jordan.

Jordan's "15 minutes" stretched into many months as news organizations avidly sought his opinions. For *Newsday*, April 28, 2002, he wrote:

"[T]he Catholic church has long been both loudly homophobic and intensely homoerotic. ... Pious young men struggling with homoerotic desires are still attracted to seminaries and religious houses of study. Why? ... We have long found a home in this church because many of its symbols and roles, its beauties and gifts, are so evidently our own."

Jordan also has examined sexuality in Christianity through many articles and three other books. (See "From Projects to Publications," page 77.)

Mark D. Jordan
Ph.D., University of Texas at Austin
Asa Griggs Candler Professor of Religion, Emory University
CSLR Senior Fellow

For me, as a scholar working on the history of sexual ethics, the real question wasn't "What happened then?" but "How does what happened then influence what happens now?" John Witte's invitation to join his project on sex, marriage, and family created the perfect moment for me, because I was ready to enter a much broader conversation about contemporary debates—legal, political, sociological, medical—and to connect with what other scholars were doing.

To describe Mark Jordan's scholarly output in a single word, try "bold." Jordan himself attributes some of that quality to his association with the CSLR. "Being a fellow in the Center," he says, "has emboldened me to do all kinds of work I would not have done otherwise—to take up some questions that were a real stretch for me." Some of those questions have stretched the public mind as well. In numerous books and articles, Jordan has broached volatile topics ranging from historic Christian teachings on sex, the relationship between Christian theology and power, and issues of homosexuality—including same-sex marriages—in Christian churches. Awards for his teaching and research include a prestigious Guggenheim Fellowship.

THE TESTIMONY OF EXPERTS

Deep into their individual research, Center scholars also did their part in keeping relevant issues before the public. Throughout the project, major news organizations—*The New York Times, The Washington Post, The Christian Science Monitor*—tapped Witte and Browning, as well as CSLR Senior Fellows Michael Broyde, Steven M. Tipton, Robert Franklin, Carol J. Hogue, and others for commentary on marriage-related topics.

Unless [the church's] process of discernment involves women and those who are married, then neither the teaching on sex and marriage nor the integrity and credibility of the clergy can hope for much improvement.

Luke Timothy Johnson
"Currie Lecture in Law and Religion" 2002

And, there was no shortage of public forums on the subject. Early in the project, February 2001, Witte delivered "An Apt and Cheerful Conversation on Marriage" for the university's Distinguished Faculty Lecture, followed by a Kessler Reformation Lecture in October 2002 on "The Perils of Celibacy: Clerical Marriage and the Protestant Reformation." That same month, CSLR Senior Fellow Luke T. Johnson spoke on "Sex and American Catholics" for Emory's annual Currie Lecture in Law and Religion. And for the 2002 Decalogue Lecture, Jordan previewed his in-progress book—later published as *Blessing Same-Sex Unions*. In a combined public lecture and panel discussion, March 2002, Atlanta family law attorney John C. Mayoue and three scholars from the project—Broyde, Timothy Jackson, and Hogue—shared a conversation on "Legal and Ethical Issues Surrounding Frozen Embryos." Mayoue returned to the stage in January 2007 to moderate "The Future of Marriage and Family Life," showcasing the research findings of Jordan, Witte, Anita Bernstein, and Karen Worthington.

Through these forums and others—which were webcasted and published as DVDs—the Center heightened the public awareness and highlighted the tangled complexity of many controversial issues surrounding sex, marriage, and family.

Witte said, "We are summoning our resources and getting our religious communities in all their diversity to deal with the hardest questions modern society is asking: What goes on in the womb and before? Where do you define the edges of marriage and non-marriage? In what form and forum can sexuality best be expressed and disciplined?" (*Emory Magazine,* Winter 2003).

The message to the thousands who participated in these forums was plain and persistent: "Our most basic societal structure, the family, stands in confusion and turmoil. It's time for religion to weigh in—and to help find ways out. We believe that with a lot of honest self-assessment, it can."

In March 2003, the project's ambitious international conference suggested, *Here's how.*

ANCIENT WISDOM, CREATIVE ADAPTATION

March 2003: Riding the crest of the previous two years' collective research and public witness, the Center hosted a major international conference, "Sex, Marriage, and Family & the Religions of the Book: Modern Problems, Enduring Solutions."

Martin Marty called this gathering "a cosmic conference," and it's easy to see why. The roster of distinguished presenters reads like an honor roll of public intellectuals, policy-makers, and scholarly leaders. Spanning the disciplines—anthropologists, economists, ethicists, historians, jurists, primatologists, psychologists, sociologists, theologians, and public health experts—these 80 speakers also represented a multitude of religious and political perspectives. The conference attracted more than 750 participants during its three days and 35 presentations.

Among the wide range of topics discussed were covenant marriage, in-vitro fertilization, contraception, adoption, abortion, same-sex marriages, rising rates of divorce and of single, unwed mothers, the absence of African American fathers, and inter-religious marriages.

One of the most spirited sessions was the plenary panel discussion, "I Do, I Don't: The Cases For and Against Marriage."

"The panelists took on the tough issues of whether marriage should be celebrated as a community strength that makes men and women healthier and happier; abolished as a legal category that discriminates against single or cohabiting couples; maintained as a way of keeping fathers involved in childrearing; or kept as a societal control to ward off sexual chaos." (*United Methodist News Service*, April 2, 2003)

Yielding a lavish library of video and electronic resources, the conference marked a mid-point in the life of the project. It offered the scholars an opportunity to share their in-progress research and test the waters of response, and it helped them complete monographs and anthologies. (See "From Projects to Publications," page 77).

WHAT THEY SAID

"We can understand the volatility and intractability of the family debate because the family generates so much heat. It is the site of our deepest longings and most terrifying fears. Families intensify every basic human urge, from our most generous capacities to give life to and sustain others, to our most passionate desires to dominate."
Jean Bethke Elshtain
Laura Spelman Rockefeller Professor of Social and Political Ethics
University of Chicago

"The quandary is why the trend in levels of marital happiness has not improved. If more people in unhappy marriages are no longer married, then those who remain married should, on the whole, be happier than their counterparts a generation ago. This is clearly not the case."
Robert Wuthnow
Gerhard R. Andlinger Professor of Sociology, Princeton University

"While the Bible announces that upon marriage the husband and wife become one flesh, the Qur'an does not present such a drastic view of marriage. Husband and wife are expected to live together in tranquility, affection, and mercy, but neither loses his or her independence, whether legal, social, or financial."
Azizah Y. al-Hibri
Professor of Law, University of Richmond

"Only as families leave their television and computer screens at home to participate with their neighbors and friends in religious and civic life can they find the genuine meaning of family."

Robert N. Bellah
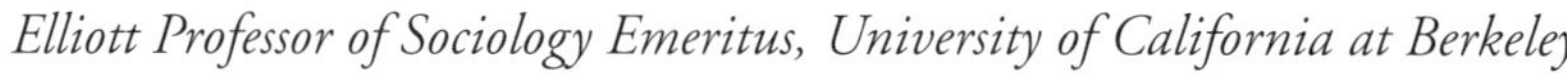
Elliott Professor of Sociology Emeritus, University of California at Berkeley

"People are uncomfortable with forced equality. The most stable relationships, research has found, are those in which one spouse does do more than their share (of the housework), but the other spouse makes up for it in other ways."
Margaret F. Brinig
Professor of Family Law, University of Iowa

"If the family is the foundation of public life, and if it has become weak, every structure in civic society will become weaker—or will it? Much work will have to be done to re-imagine family, religion, and education."
Rebecca S. Chopp
President, Colgate University

FROM PROJECTS TO PUBLICATIONS

Sex, Marriage, and Family research involves continuing analysis of the role that Christianity, Judaism, and Islam have played and can play in forming and reforming theories, laws, and practices of sex, marriage, and family life. A selection of the project's many side-projects and published volumes appears below.

SELECTED PROJECTS

Same-Sex Unions, Same-Sex Marriage (2001 - 2005)
An exploration of the range of arguments about same-sex union and marriage within canonical traditions, religious communities, modern societies, and the modern state.
Highlights: conference; roundtable conferences; four books

Sex, Marriage, and Family in the World Religions (2002 - 2005)
Analysis of the enduring teachings of the major religions on sex, marriage, and family, and their interactions with modern law and culture.
Highlights: roundtable conferences; two books

I Do, I Don't: The Cases For and Against Marriage (2002 - 2005)
Analysis and illustration of the modern American debate about the legal status and forms of marriage.
Highlights: roundtable conference; one book

The Modern Family in Interdisciplinary Perspective (2003 - 2005)
An interdisciplinary study of the shifting principles, policies, and practices of the modern family in America and abroad.
Highlights: roundtable conference; one book

Marrying in the Middle Ages (2003 - 2006)
Analysis of the legal, religious, and social forms and norms of marriage from late antiquity to the early Reformation era.
Highlights: roundtable conference; one book

SELECTED PUBLICATIONS

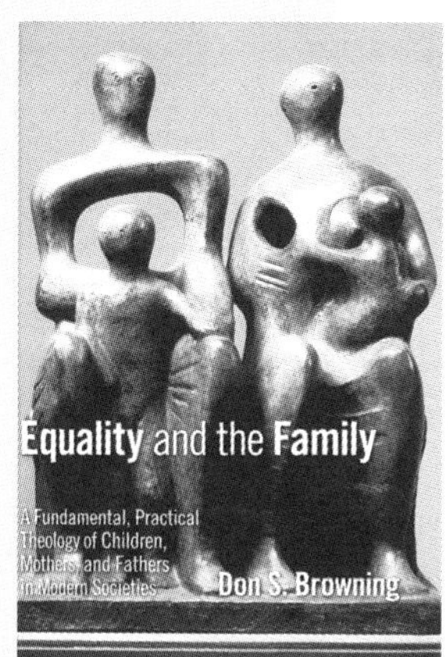

Don S. Browning, *Equality and the Family* (Wm. B. Eerdmans, 2007)
Theologian and social scientist Browning hopes to improve children's lives and nudge modern families toward well-being by instilling a new vision of what "family" can mean. This book presents the key: a marriage founded on "equal regard," a covenant relationship in which both husband and wife consider each other as equals, treat each other with respectful concern, work together to ensure equitable responsibilities and privileges, and raise their children to sustain such relationships as well.

Don S. Browning, *Marriage and Modernization: How Globalization Threatens Marriage and What to Do about It* (Wm. B. Eerdmans, 2003)
It's another big question, and a global one: How can marriage be renewed—worldwide? Modernization has helped nudge marriage into its current state, Browning explains, and now it's time for religion, specifically Christianity, to help create a practical new vision.

Michael J. Broyde and Michael Ausubel, eds., *Marriage, Sex, and Family in Judaism* (Rowman and Littlefield, 2005)
Through scholarly essays that present its multilayered historical and legal traditions, the Jewish family emerges in its fascinating complexity. The collection proves, as its preface asserts, that "the way [the Jewish family] is does not need to be the way it always will be or the way it always was."

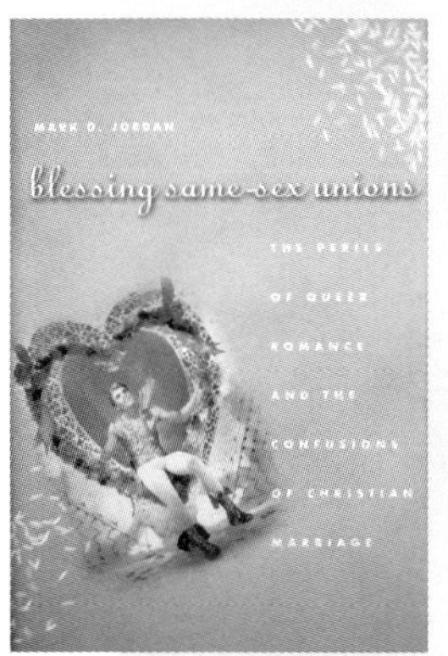

Mark D. Jordan, *Blessing Same-Sex Unions: The Perils of Queer Romance and the Confusions of Christian Marriage* (University of Chicago Press, 2005)
Carefully selected ideals of Christian marriage have come to dominate recent debates over same-sex unions. No matter what the courts do, argues Jordan, Christian churches will have to decide for themselves whether these unions deserve and receive blessing.

Steven M. Tipton and John Witte, Jr., eds., *Family Transformed: Religion, Values, and Society in American Life* (Georgetown University Press, 2005)
This volume offers multifaceted analysis of a complex institution, gathering an array of experts—outstanding scholars from the fields of anthropology, demography, ethics, history, law, philosophy, primatology, and psychology.

Abdullahi Ahmed An-Na'im, ed. *Inter-religious Marriages Among Muslims: Negotiating Religious Identity in Family and Community* (Global Media Publications, 2005)

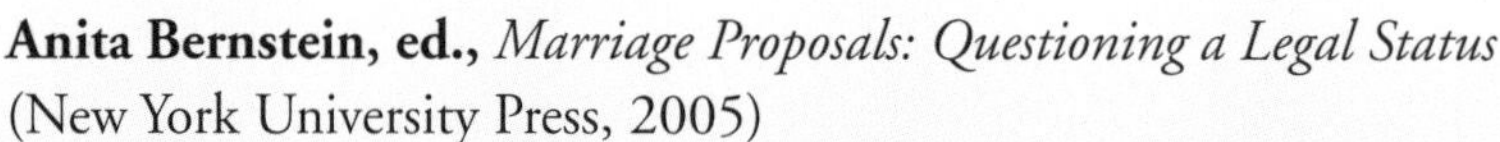

Anita Bernstein, ed., *Marriage Proposals: Questioning a Legal Status* (New York University Press, 2005)

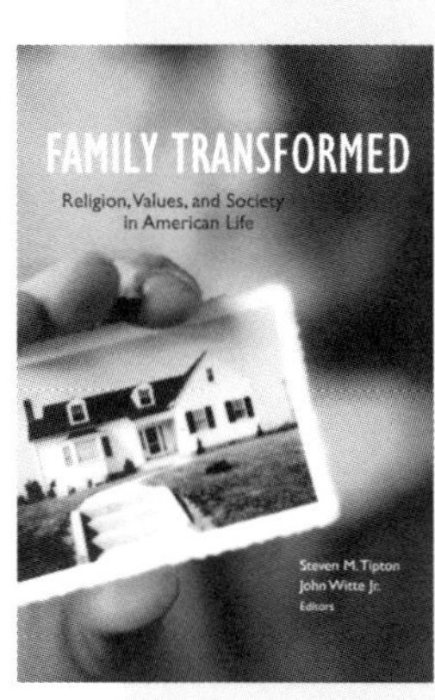

Don S. Browning and David Clairmont, eds., *American Religions and the Family: How Faith Traditions Cope with Modernization and Democracy* (Columbia University Press, 2006)

Don S. Browning, M. Christian Green, and John Witte, Jr., eds., *Sex, Marriage and Family in the World Religions* (Columbia University Press, 2005)

Mark D. Jordan, ed., *Authorizing Marriage? Canon, Tradition, and Critique in the Blessing of Same-Sex Unions* (Princeton University Press, 2006)

Cynthia B. Patterson, ed., *Antigone's Answer: Death, Burial and Commemoration in Sophocles' Athens* (Helios Journal, 2006)

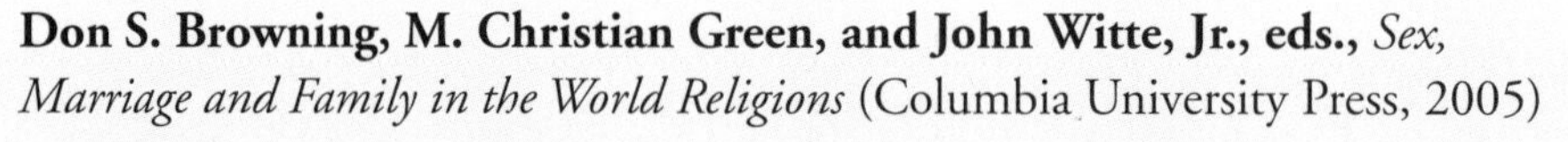

Philip L. Reynolds and John Witte, Jr., eds., *To Have and to Hold: Marrying and Its Documentation in Western Christendom, 400-1600* (Cambridge University Press, 2007)

John Witte, Jr. and Eliza Ellison, eds., *Covenant Marriage in Comparative Perspective* (Wm. B. Eerdmans, 2005)

John Witte, Jr., M. Christian Green, and Amy Wheeler, *The Equal Regard Family and its Friendly Critics: Don Browning and the Practical Theological Ethics of the Family* (Wm. B. Eerdmans, 2007)

John Witte, Jr. and Robert M. Kingdon, eds., *Sex, Marriage, and Family in John Calvin's Geneva I: Courtship, Engagement, Marriage* (Wm. B. Eerdmans, 2005)

A complete listing of projects and books is available at www.law.emory.edu/cslr.

FOR WORSE, FOR BETTER

An argument, noted Martin Marty in the final presentation of the 2003 conference, is something you can win or lose. A conversation, in contrast, is something people create together, something everyone can learn from, and can put to good use.

Despite bleak statistics, entrenched societal patterns, and the predictably plodding pace of change, the Center's ongoing project on sex, marriage, and family bears a legacy of hope. Transitioning naturally to the next project, a study of the child—this complex project seeded, just as the family itself always does, the possibility of new and better families ahead.

Faced with the gloomy version of tomorrow—the many children now growing up abused, fatherless, delinquent—Marty didn't try to argue it away. Instead, he did what heroes in the old stories have always done. He posed a new question.

"But where do all the good kids come from? And what do you mean by 'good'? And if you find out, what do you do with the knowledge?"

He paused. "Ah," he continued, "we're already in the middle of the next conversation."

THE MYSTERY OF CHILDREN: WHO SHOULD KEEP WATCH?

A standing *problem*, one foot firmly planted in law and another foot in religion, is typically how the Center's interdisciplinary research has begun. The 2003-2007 project "The Child in Law, Religion, and Society," directed by Martin Marty and John Witte, altered that pattern.

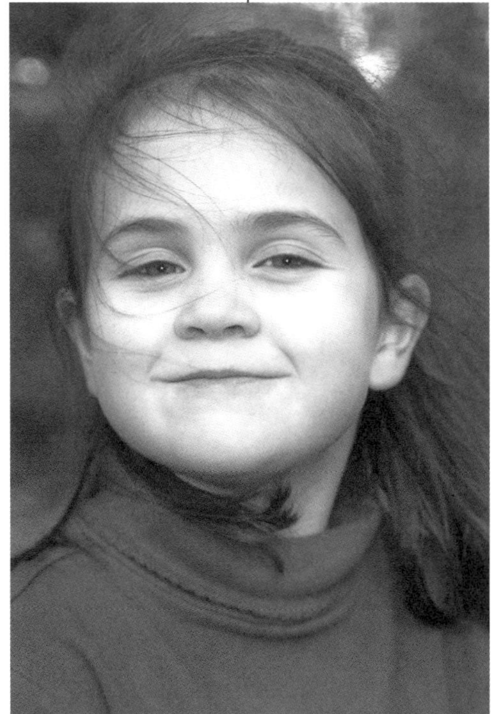

Marty recalls, "John Witte and Don Browning approached me one day. 'We have a new project and we'd like you to take part in it, and if you took part in it, what would your research focus be?' And I instantly blurted out, because I'd always cared about it, 'I'd like to work on the *mystery* of the child.'"

As The Child scholars crossed disciplines at the faculty seminar; as they examined the plights and possibilities of children at the Family Forum Series public lectures; and as they debated children's rights at the October 2005 international conference, Marty's own heartening take on the perceived "problem" of children was their guide. The opening page of his 2007 book *The Mystery of the Child* sums up his thesis: "The provision of care for children will proceed on a radically revised and improved basis if instead of seeing the child first as a problem faced with a complex set of problems, we see her as a mystery surrounded by mystery."

The Child: not a problem, then, but a mystery. And in light of this mystery, *who should keep watch?* Marty's first page takes care of that question as well: "Providing care for the child is the business of the whole society, which means that it involves all the citizens—parents and teachers, nurses and doctors, coaches and tutors, pastors and religious educators, attorneys and judges, politicians and artists, entertainers and theorists."

Then Marty goes a decisive step farther. Beyond redefining the issue at hand, and beyond enlisting every adult under the sun on its behalf, he slices through any ambiguity about the issue's accompanying task. All of these diverse caretakers of children, he declares, must act from the deep core of the word *provide*, which from its Latin roots, *pro + videre*, entails "seeing forward." "The responsible provider," says Marty, "is a foreseer who arranges to supply what is needed or will be needed in the future."

The two dozen foreseers who joined The Child project in 2003 considered Marty's illumined terms, and their work evinced a compatibly visionary spirit.

Martin E. Marty
Ph.D., University of Chicago
Fairfax M. Cone Distinguished Service Professor Emeritus, University of Chicago
Robert W. Woodruff Visiting Professor of Interdisciplinary Religious Studies, Emory University

These two zones of life—law and religion—are locked together. And plenty of places in the United States have good individual scholars of this combined field, but nowhere other than the Center here at Emory can you find this convergence, this concentration of energies. That's what has always excited me about this place. Even decades ago, you could see that the momentum was building up here, that this was a place where important work could happen.

Called by *Time* magazine the nation's "most influential interpreter of religion," Martin Marty well deserves the accolades that festoon his long and productive life. If you consider his more than 50 books (including a National Book Award winner and several classics in American religious history), his more than 4,300 articles and essays, and, each year, 100 or so talks and speeches, writes Kerry Temple in *University of Chicago Magazine*, "you have a scribe/writer/wordsmith of near-mythic profusion. Maybe 400,000 published words a year."

The Center was honored to have Marty in residence, as a visiting Woodruff Professor, for the 2003-2004 academic year, when he and Witte co-directed the project on The Child in Law, Religion, and Society and also hosted the CSLR Family Forum Series. "Never before," says Witte, "have I encountered a scholar with such boundless and bracing energy, or such a lively and learned pen."

Recently retired as senior editor of *The Christian Century*, Marty is past president of the American Academy of Religion, the American Society of Church History, and—surprisingly, for a Lutheran—the American Catholic Historical Association. For 35 years he taught at the University of Chicago, where the Martin Marty Center has been founded to promote "public religion" endeavors.

Over the years, Marty has served on two U.S. Presidential Commissions and directed both the Fundamentalism Project of the American Academy of Arts and Sciences and the Public Religion Project at the University of Chicago. Along the way, he has received 72 honorary doctorates. His honors include the National Humanities Medal, the Medal of the American Academy of Arts and Sciences, the University of Chicago Alumni Medal, the Distinguished Service Medal of the Association of Theological Schools, and the Order of Lincoln Medallion (Illinois' top honor).

Longstanding prominence as a public intellectual and historian has made Marty a familiar name; his debonair bow-tie and his habitual look of merriment make him a happily familiar face as well. Labeled a "phenomenon" by his friend Bill Moyers, Marty says simply that he'd most like to be remembered as a good teacher. "That's been my great joy, where I've always gotten the most pleasure."

LOOKING BACK, SEEING FORWARD

Back in 1997, *Newsweek* magazine carried a major story on this country's "lost children"—those born in poverty and in broken households, more likely than not to drop out of school, out of step, and then out of society altogether. At the time, the number of those children exceeded 15 million, and the story predicted that in two decades, unless states and churches, agencies and academies gave children a new priority, the number would double. The Child project placed that priority before a broad public audience.

In recent decades, formal theological discourse has neglected many crises among our country's children, leaving them to the province of the health, social, and public policy sciences. To help rebalance the scale, the Center set about reviewing the main contributions that religions have made—and might make—to a robust comparative theology and ethics of the child. Its scholars sought not simply to consider these little people as vulnerable victims or sobering statistics, but to focus on "children qua children," in their being and becoming, in their birth and growth.

The new project arose naturally from the work of its predecessor, "Sex, Marriage, and Family & the Religions of the Book"—whose wide-ranging seminar sessions on every element of family life had often ended with the almost-overlooked question: *What does this mean for children?*

Marty, in residence at Emory to co-direct The Child project, stated from the outset his intention to raise big, multifaceted questions that scholars of all disciplines would find relevant to their research. Participants gathered around the table once again, and the weekly buzz of querying, exchanging, and refining resumed. "Four or five of the faculty had already taken part in projects in that very room, so they didn't have to start from scratch," Marty recalls. "I think I brought a kind of ornery spirit. With this kind of pursuit, you've got to be relentless."

The project's emerging roster of research topics stretched across academic disciplines and forged some intriguing new alliances: Frank Alexander's interest in children and housing, and the impact of laws on the housing of America's families. Michael Broyde's study of Jewish tradition and the technological selection of embryos and designer babies. An in-depth inquiry by Mary E. Odem, CSLR senior fellow and associate professor of history and women's studies, on how Central American and Mexican children fare in migrant families. Senior Fellows E. Brooks Holifield and Mary Elizabeth Moore's exploration of the spiritual formation of children.

Public sharing of the scholars' evolving projects quickly followed suit.

E. Brooks Holifield
Ph.D., Yale University
Charles Howard Candler Professor of American Church History,
Emory University
CSLR Senior Fellow

While Brooks Holifield teaches, writes, and lectures widely in his specialties—religious history, the history of Christian thought in America, and early colonial American religion—his published works reveal a love of other disciplines as well. They include numerous articles, along with books on 17th-century Puritanism, the antebellum South, religion and psychology in America, health and medicine in the Methodist traditions, and America's early colonial cultural history. Among the precursors to his 2007 volume *God's Ambassadors: A History of the Christian Clergy in America* are *Theology in America: Christian Thought from the Age of the Puritans to the Civil War* and *Era of Persuasion: American Thought and Culture, 1521-1680.*

Mary Elizabeth Moore
Ph.D., Claremont Graduate University
Director, Program for Women in Theology and Ministry
Professor of Religion and Education, Emory University
CSLR Senior Fellow

Children who live under difficult circumstances yearn for wholeness, believes Mary Elizabeth Moore, and her forthcoming volume, *Yearnings and Hopes: Eschatological Visions of Youth*, supports her conviction. In this and previous writings, Moore explores practical theology with a particular concern for *tikkun olam,* "repair of the world"—an act that each person can participate in, thus partnering with God. Her research spans eco-feminist theology and spirituality, cultural contexts and theological perspectives of youth, sacramental teaching, reconciliation theory and practice, and theologies of the Wesleyan tradition. She also serves as the English co-editor of the *International Journal of Practical Theology.* Her recent books include *Teaching from the Heart, Ministering with the Earth; Covenant and Call*; and *Teaching as a Sacramental Act.*

CONVERSATIONS FOR CHANGE: THE FAMILY FORUM SERIES ON CHILDREN

Like the Chinese character for *change*, the public component of The Child project encompassed both crisis and opportunity. Launched in 2003, the Family Forum Series lectures and panel discussions addressed crises—phrased in poignant questions—that afflict the lives of 21st-century children. Marty, the consummate host, served variously as interviewer, moderator, and respondent. For each event, the Law School's Tull Auditorium attracted a full house.

"Who Cares for the Children?" asked the opening session on September 2003. Martha A. Fineman, Robert W. Woodruff Professor of Law at Emory, CSLR senior fellow, and an acclaimed expert in family law and feminist theory, said that to fight child poverty effectively in the U.S., the state should exert more care, supplying guaranteed child support and child allowances for every family. Afterward, Browning agreed that the problem requires radical social reform and presented his theory of the "equal-regard" family as a means of providing the best possible environment for children.

Other programs in the year's series brought esteemed visitors to campus. In October, "Children: Will We Ever Get It Right?" featured William H. Foege, former director of the Centers for Disease Control and Prevention, past executive director of The Carter Center, Presidential Distinguished Service Professor Emeritus at Emory, and a fellow and advisor to the Bill and Melinda Gates Foundation. Highlighting the plight of poor children around the world and the role America should play in alleviating it, Foege acknowledged both progress and problem: "What's happened to children and health around the world is unbelievable improvement and unbelievable inequities," he said.

Millard Fuller, founder and president of Habitat for Humanity International, addressed in February 2004 the question "Where Do the Children Live?" In a subsequent op-ed article, Marty described Fuller as "a realist full of hope": "Dr. Fuller, a master storyteller, told the audience of numerous incidents in which a child of poverty found life changed, thanks to the dignity and comfort of the simple home" that Habitat volunteers provided.

The Family Forum Series, 2003-2007, is available on webcast at www.law.emory.edu/cslr.

THE CARTER CHALLENGE

Conversation led to momentous challenge during the season's showpiece, the visit of former U.S. President Jimmy Carter in October 2003. A huge crowd jammed into Tull Auditorium, listening to Carter and interviewer Marty explore what proved to be a volatile question: "What Happens to Children in Peril?" Carter pointed to the ever-growing chasm between the world's rich and poor as the most profound threat to children today. Extreme poverty, he said, causes "despair and hopelessness, and eventually alienation and anger that sometimes leads to violence."

> The President set out to unsettle academics, including his interviewer and those involved with the project on The Child, that they might reach beyond the mere study and writing of books and articles.
>
> **Martin E. Marty**
> CSLR op-ed article, 2003

Carter called to account the United States—"the wealthiest and the greatest nation in the world"—for its low ranking in foreign aid; for its criminal justice system "grossly biased" toward rich, white, affluent people such as himself; and particularly for its refusal to sign the United Nations Convention on the Rights of the Child.

Seriously but without rancor, Carter persisted, "What is the Emory Law School going to do about these problems? What are its individual deans or students going to do? I would guess, nothing. I've seen, hundreds of times, how think tanks and major universities analyze a problem and write beautiful books on what was said. I hope and pray that out of this forum will come not just advice and analysis, but some tangible means to alleviate the problems of the children of the world. If that were done, it would send reverberations throughout the legal profession."

The glove had been thrown. And as they joined in the applause, the leaders of the Center knew that the next move was theirs.

ONE CENTER'S FIRST RESPONSE

Plans for The Child project had always included a major conference, but Carter's challenge decided its direction. In October 2005, a crowd of some 500 conferees gathered at Emory Law School to debate the question "What's Wrong with Rights for Children?"—and specifically to exchange perspectives on the failure of the United States to ratify the UN Convention on the Rights of the Child.

Although the United States played a leading role in drafting the Children's Convention, and although early signs suggested that the U.S. Senate might provide its consent, several questions arose about the merits of the document, and it was never sent to the Senate for a vote.

At the conference, convened by CSLR Senior Fellows T. Jeremy Gunn of the American Civil Liberties Union, and Johan D. van der Vyver, I.T. Cohen Professor of International Law and Human Rights, the conversation expanded to include a score of leading churchmen and statesmen, litigators and legislators, jurists and ethicists, UN officials and NGO advocates. The resulting discussion raised questions of its own:

Is rights talk the right talk for talking about the special needs and concerns, interests and aspirations, callings and duties of children? If not, why not?

Is the 1989 UN Convention on the Rights of the Child the best modern formulation of children's rights? What's missing? What's misinformed? What's been misinterpreted?

Should the United States ratify the Convention—especially having worked so hard to shape many of its 54 articles, and especially since all other countries besides Somalia (which has no government) have ratified it? What have been the obstacles and objections to American ratification?

How have other countries fared who have ratified the Convention, and what comparative legal and cultural lessons might they offer us in protecting children who are the most voiceless, voteless, and vulnerable amongst us?

In addition to the keynote addresses from Carter and Marty, the two-day conference featured five panel discussions among distinguished experts from North America and Western Europe: "What Does the Children's Convention Require?"; "Why Did the U.S. Drive the Children's Convention and Then Withdraw Support?"; "What's Wrong with Children's Rights?"; "How Would States Apply the Children's Convention?"; and "Should Religious Groups Oppose the Children's Convention?" (See webcasts at www.law.emory.edu/cslr.)

A month after the conference, Marty summed up its proceedings in an article for *Emory Report* (November 28, 2005): "Most of the contributors to the October conference regarded the United States' failure to ratify to be a diplomatic mistake, a misreading of the document, or the product of an overheated domestic atmosphere, all of which combined to derail the intended result: the ratification and employment of the Convention in domestic life and international affairs."

So why did the U.S. object to the document? Conferees cited a number of reasons: originally, the desire to protect states' rights to execute children under 18 years of age; subsequently, the country's sovereign distaste for signing treaties (including the Kyoto Global Warming Agreement, nuclear arms agreements, and international human rights agreements), along with some religious groups' conviction that the authority of the father, as the inviolate head of the household, would be undermined by rights of children—despite the Convention's "escape clause" asserting parents' rights to guide and discipline a child.

Although Carter used the stark word "hopeless" to describe the possibility that the United States would join the rest of the world in ratifying the document, he urged conference participants to "work together as enthusiastically and individually and collectively as possible to implement the non-controversial provisions of the Convention"—which, in itself, is a far from hopeless case.

"Meanwhile," came the last word from Marty, "if the United States keeps erring by failing to support [the Convention], Carter and most conference participants will keep pointing at all that can be accomplished in its generous name and spirit."

WHAT THEY SAID

"Let me be blunt about it. I don't see any chance in the near future, maybe in the lifetime of some of us, for the United States to ratify the UN Convention unless there is a provision in it of non-applicability to the United States."
Former U.S. President Jimmy Carter

"The most fundamental requirement is that the child is recognized and fully respected as a human being with rights."
Professor Jaap Doek
Chair, UN Committee on the Rights of the Child

"Our countries share a common perception of the family as a protected area. Too many people in North America simply do not believe that children should have rights."
The Honorable Landon Pearson
The Senate of Canada

"BUT HOW ARE YOU GOING TO CHANGE THE WORLD?"

More than once, Carter has pushed this question with audiences at Emory, insisting that if research ends only with 19 more books in the library, little is actually accomplished. What's needed, he says, is active, hands-on helping. Marty cites one instance when Carter, having asked his pointed question, actually pulled out a calendar and read off the projects for which he needed immediate assistance, such as helping the homeless and prostitutes. And it worked. "A month later," says Marty, "a student told me, 'I never did anything like that before, but a former president asked me to—so I did. Now I'm hooked.'"

The Child project, with its figurative and literal "19 books"—and counting: how will it generate change? In a 2007 interview with the Center, Marty offered a confident response: "If Frank Alexander goes back to Flint, Michigan, where he studies the laws for the homeless and draws together 10 or 20 people who deal with homeless children and families elsewhere, they're going to change the world. And if our books are ones that teachers read and then teach, or that parents read and then talk about with their friends, these books will change the world, too."

Toward productive change—over the long haul, if not overnight—the scholars of The Child project have set about producing some of the books that may spark new thinking, which itself is the beginning of new behavior.

Potentially world changing? The scholars of the Center, their students, and their readers in many professions—who turn over these new ideas, then turn them outward into new ways of being and doing—like to think so.

FROM PROJECTS TO PUBLICATIONS

The Child in Law, Religion, and Society has generated inquiry into a wide assortment of topics in which concerns related to children, law, religion, and society converge. Listed below is a selection of projects and volumes.

PROJECTS

The Child in World Religions (2003 -)
Analysis of the nurture, education, and formation of children in the world religions, and in America.
Highlights: roundtable conferences, two books

What's Wrong with Rights for Children? (2004 -)
Examination of the legal, political, social, and thematic arguments for and against children's rights in general, and their formulation in the 1989 UN Convention on the Rights of the Child in particular.
Highlights: conferences in the U.S., Ireland, and South Africa, journal symposium, book

The Vocation of the Child in Comparative Christian Perspectives (2004 -   )
An analysis of historical and contemporary Christian formulations of the duties or vocation of the child.
Highlights: two roundtable conferences, one book

Children, Youth, and Spirituality in a Troubled World (2004 -   )
A practical theological analysis of the spiritual yearning, expressions, and challenges of children and youth in the present world of rapid change, dislocation, violence, and competing loyalties.
Highlights: conference, one book

The Best Love of the Child (2005 -   )
A comparative analysis of the "best interest of the child" principle in law and the "best love of the child" principle in theology and the social sciences, with an argument that the first right of the child is the right to be loved.
Highlights: roundtable conferences, one book

SELECTED PUBLICATIONS

Timothy P. Jackson, *The Morality of Adoption: Social-Psychological, Theological, and Legal Perspectives* (Wm. B. Eerdmans, 2005)
A belief that the sanctity rights of needy children deserve special attention led ethicist Jackson to gather the scholarly essays that make up this volume. "My goal for the book was not only to help clarify thinking on these very complex issues, but to move people to act," he says.

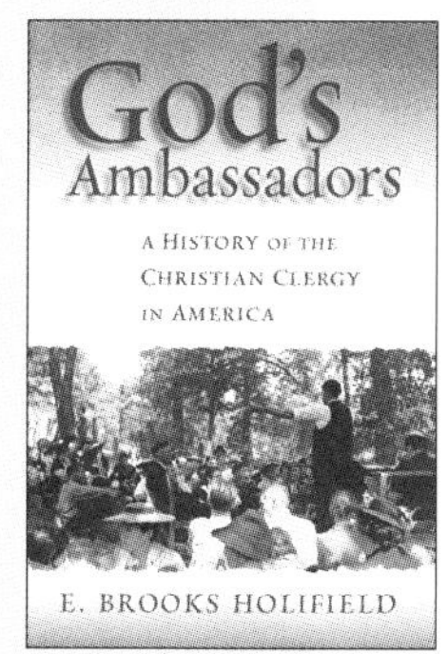

E. Brooks Holifield, *God's Ambassadors: A History of the Christian Clergy in America* (Wm. B. Eerdmans, 2007)
Church historian Holifield examines the varied and changing roles of priests and ministers over three centuries. Along the way, he gives attention to roles that specifically involve children, such as overseeing children's spiritual formation, teaching children and youth in Sunday school, and establishing recreational ministries.

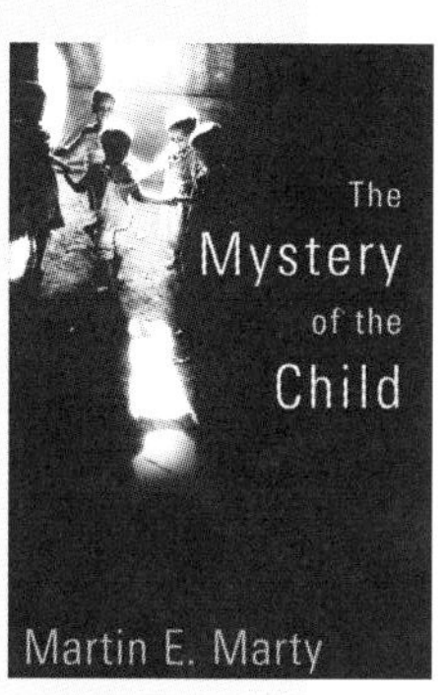

Martin E. Marty, *The Mystery of the Child* (Wm. B. Eerdmans, 2007)
Readers of this volume, the culmination of Marty's work with The Child project, will never be able to think of childhood—or, for that matter, adulthood—in exactly the same way again. "Martin Marty encourages all of us to maintain the child's openness to wonder as we grow old," explained Bill Moyers, introducing Marty on *Bill Moyers Journal.* During the program, which aired August 2007 on public broadcasting stations throughout the country, Marty commented that when you think of children as mystery, "you're drawn into seeing the world in their angle." And when you spend your life finding ways to change and become like a little child, as Jesus advised, he added, "you will be more open to mystery, more responsive to others, more receptive."

Frank S. Alexander, *Housing and Families: The Mirrors of Law* (forthcoming)

Don S. Browning, *Christian Ethics and the Moral Psychologies* (Wm. B. Eerdmans, 2006)

Don S. Browning and Bonnie Miller-McLemore, eds., *Children and Childhood in American Religions* (Rutgers University Press, 2008)

Don S. Browning and Marcia Bunge, eds., *The Child in World Religions* (Rutgers University Press, 2008)

John E. Coons and Patrick M. Brennan, eds., *The Vocation of the Child* (Wm. B. Eerdmans, forthcoming)

M. Christian Green, *Fatherhood and Feminism: Justice, Care, and Gender in the Family* (forthcoming)

Carol and Lynn Hogue, *Sex in the Dark: What is Responsible Con(tra)ception?* (forthcoming)

Timothy P. Jackson, *The Best Love of the Child in Theological, Ethical, and Legal Perspectives* (forthcoming)

Mark D. Jordan, *Queer Adolescence in Christian America* (University of Chicago Press, 2009)

Mary Elizabeth Moore, *Children, Youth, and Spirituality in a Troubled World* (Louis Chalice Press, 2008)

Mary Elizabeth Moore, *Teaching as a Sacramental Act* (Pilgrim, 2004)

Mary Elizabeth Moore, ed., *Yearnings and Hopes: Eschatological Visions of Youth* (forthcoming)

Mary E. Odem, *Mexican Immigration to the U.S. Southeast: Impact and Challenges* (Instituto de Mexico, 2005)

Philip L. Reynolds, *Parental Goods: Medieval Theology and Beyond* (forthcoming)

John Witte, Jr., ed., "What's Wrong with Rights for Children?," *Emory International Law Review* 20 (2006): 1-239

John Witte, Jr., *The Sins of the Fathers: The Law and Theology of Illegitimacy Reconsidered* (Cambridge University Press, 2008)

A complete listing of projects and books is available at www.law.emory.edu/cslr.

CAUSE FOR HOPE

Faith is a loyal wife,
Charity is a fervent mother,
But hope is a very little girl ...

It is faith who holds fast through century upon century.

It is charity who gives herself through centuries of centuries,
But it is my little hope
Who gets up every morning ...

Charles Péguy, *The Mystery of the Holy Innocents*
quoted by Martin Marty, *The Mystery of the Child*

Every project undertaken by the Center for the Study of Law and Religion has given witness to three convictions: Change is needed. Change is possible. Research and conversation can open the way. In short, hope exists.

The project on The Child in Law, Religion, and Society began, as usual, with a problem. It raised questions, stimulating scholars to raise their own. Then, through the vision of two prominent figures, Carter and Marty, it received a fresh perspective.

Holding up a concern for children—their plights, rights, and promise—the Center's scholars are literally *providing*, "seeing forward" beyond the problems to what can be in the lives of these little ones. The next step requires seeing even further forward, to what can be in the life of anyone who learns to see through the eyes of a child, and to a new understanding of how that seeing can yield significant change.

From the project on The Child, all of us have much to learn about the mystery of children, the necessity of hope, the meaning of change, and the uneasy bond between religion and law. The Center continues to keep watch.

And he said: "I tell you the truth, unless you change and become like little children, you will never enter the kingdom of heaven."

Matthew 18:3

I believe that only a shared faith in the common destiny of mankind will provide the vision and the support necessary to the continued creation of a world order governed by law, and that a belief in world law is necessary to provide the vision and the support necessary to the establishment of a world religion.

Harold J. Berman
Robert W. Woodruff Professor of Law, Emory University

IN THE FUTURE

LAW AND RELIGION IN THE AGE OF THE HOLY SPIRIT

Harold J. Berman

The main challenge to law and religion studies at Emory in the next quarter century, in my view, is to broaden their primary focus from the theistic religions and their respective cultures (Judaism, Christianity, Islam) to include the interaction of law and religion not only in the other great theological traditions (Buddhism, Taoism, Hinduism, Bahai, Confucianism, and others), but also in powerful civil religions, and ideologies, such as certain forms of nationalism and certain forms of political ideology which have religious characteristics. This, indeed, is a formidable challenge, but in the present stage of world history, when all the major cultures of the world have come into increasingly close contact with each other, and when the word law itself has come to be seen increasingly in intercultural and interdisciplinary terms, religion, too, must be given the meaning of any fundamental belief-system for which people are willing to give their hearts and souls and, indeed, their lives.

The first quarter century of Emory's Law and Religion Center has helped to show the way to such an expansion of its vision. We have, from the start, addressed in our teaching and research, the enduring legal contributions of Judaism, Christianity, and Islam. We have explored many of the legal and religious foundations and fundamentals of democracy and human rights, proselytism and religious freedom, constitutionalism and rule of law, marriage, children, and the family.

We have not neglected, during the past quarter century, Jesus' admonition to the Pharisees, "Woe unto you lawyers, for you tithe mint and dill and cumin and neglect the weightier matters of the law, which are justice and mercy and good faith" (Matthew 23:23). We have been concerned with the responsibility of lawyers to serve justice and mercy and good faith in their relationships not only to their clients and to the local communities in which they work, but to nations of which they are a part.

PROPHETIC VOICES

Since law and religion represent profound and nearly universal realms of human existence, and since they are interactive in various ways among most people around the world, citizens are finding it important to discern new ways for law and religion to interact and, to become together a synergetic force with two sets of approaches. Thus the separate topics *"law"* and *"religion"* can be connected with hyphens into *"law-and-religion."*

Martin E. Marty
University of Chicago

COMING TOGETHER IS PROVIDENTIAL

We have not yet, however, devoted sufficient attention to the role and rule of law in the multicultural world society of which we and our local communities and our nation are a part—a world society that is gradually emerging in the 20th and 21st centuries. We live in a world economy, supported by a growing body of transnational law of trade and finance and investment. Through new technology, we also have virtually instantaneous worldwide communications, also subject to an emerging body of transnational legal regulation. Transnational organizations and associations of all kinds are formed to advance a myriad of different causes. Many of them influence legal responses to world disorder and world injustices, to pollution and destruction of the world's environment, to threats to universal human rights, to world diseases, worldwide terrorism, ethnic and religious conflict. People of the world have come together in calling for the development of worldwide legal protection against these global scourges through the development of official and unofficial legal institutions.

I do not doubt the providential character of this historical development, which is a culmination of more than 5,000 years of human history. Gradually, century by century, the peoples of the world have been brought into contact with each other. Especially in the second millennium of the Christian era, Western Christendom, through its missionaries, its merchants, and its military, made a world around itself. Now as we enter the third millennium of that history, the West is no longer the center. All humanity is joined together in a common destiny. Despite two World Wars and their aftermath of terrible ethnic, territorial, and ideological conflicts, St. Paul's extraordinary insight—that "every race of man" is "made of one blood to inhabit the whole earth's surface" (Acts 17:24, 26)—has not only been proved scientifically but has also become a historical reality. We are all faced with the alternative of worldwide mutual support or worldwide mutual destruction.

I think I speak for others in our Center in saying that I believe that this is providential. Isn't the interaction of all the peoples of the world with each other what was intended from the beginning? Isn't that what world history has been all about—that the unity of the human race should become a possibility, a challenge? I think that the God of history has put it to us squarely: Either you now come together or you will destroy each other!

PROPHETIC VOICES

There is now a broader recognition that law and legal decisions involve moral choices, and whether the law adopts, ignores or abandons a moral principle that a religion supports, it is not neutral.

Daniel G. Ashburn
J.D./M.Div.,
Emory University, 1993
Associate,
Powell Goldstein LLP

PROPHETIC VOICES

It is my hope that the future of this work and its great integrative insights will continue to lead to fresh and creative ways of resolving conflicts through frameworks that accommodate pluralism without blanching religious expression of its essence.

Charles Hooker
J.D./Ph.D. Candidate,
Emory University, 2006
Associate,
Kilpatrick Stockton LLP

WORLD ORDER IS RESPONSIBILITY OF LAWYERS

What has this to do with lawyers? Everything! As Benno Schmidt, former Dean of Columbia Law School and former President of Yale University, wrote several years ago, "The world has replaced the nation as the context within which the professions operate." Most major American law firms have offices in one or more other parts of the world, and most of the smaller firms as well have clients involved in transnational transactions of one kind or another. A world economy—world trade, world finance, world investment—cannot operate without legal rules, legal procedures, legal concepts, legal values, and these cannot be formulated and maintained and developed without the participation of the world's lawyers.

Even apart from multinational legal practice, it is the lawyer's responsibility, and the lawyer's opportunity, to help to construct a world order that is founded on justice, mercy, and good faith. Order is one part of it: rules, precedents, consistency, predictability are one side of law; like cases should be decided alike; people should be able to calculate the legal consequences of their acts. The other part of it is justice: equality, fairness, trust, due process, both substantive and procedural—not just the rules but the larger purposes of the rules. I referred earlier to Jesus' profound words: "Woe unto you lawyers, for you tithe mint and dill and cumin"—that is, you keep order and enforce the technicalities—"but you neglect the weightier matters of the law, which are justice, and mercy, and good faith—you should do that without neglecting the others!"

GOLDEN RULE A GLOBAL ETHIC

I take it to be a principal challenge to our Center to study various aspects of the dependence of the body of world law on the development of a common belief-system among the various cultures of the world, cultures which do not share the same theologies and the same concepts of law but which are increasingly challenged to share a commitment to build a world order founded on a universal sense of justice and mercy and good faith.

Let me speak first about common features of the world's religions, and then about common features of the world's legal systems, and finally about the kind of faith that is needed to forge a relationship between the two.

The great religions of the world, while they differ from each other in their theology and their metaphysics, share certain moral principles; they have a common ethic. All the great religions affirm the Golden Rule—that you should do unto others what you would want others to do unto you, that you should love your neighbor, that you should aid those who are in distress. All proclaim that the dignity of all persons should be respected, that every human being should be treated humanely, that persons should not lie but should speak truthfully, that one should not murder, that one should not steal, that one should not bear false witness against another. Indeed, anthropologists have shown that in all the cultures of the world, including the most primitive, there are moral rules corresponding to the last six of the Biblical Ten Commandments. Since 1993, thousands of religious leaders from around the world have met periodically in a Parliament of the World's Religions, which has adopted a Declaration of a Global Ethic affirming a fundamental consensus among all the world's religions on binding values and irrevocable moral standards.

PROPHETIC VOICES

As we seek moral guidance and religious meaning, we will not be able simply to invoke precedents from times past, for our ancestors could never have even imagined our world, let alone taught us about how to live nobly in it. We instead will need to draw on the deep convictions of our religious and secular traditions and give them new meaning as we apply them to our new world.

Elliot Dorff
American Hebrew University

There are, of course, within each of the denominations, extremists who would confine the Golden Rule and other related moral obligations to those who share their own narrower version of their denominational doctrine. There are among adherents of all religions advocates of intolerance against those who disagree with their interpretation of the true doctrine. Yet these are perversions of authentic religion, which reduce its essential postulate of universality to parochial dogmas and parochial interests.

All the great religions are expressions of a fundamental need of sociability that is inherent in human nature, and it is that inclination that is a fundamental source of all law. Indeed, the great 17th-century founder of modern international law, Hugo Grotius, rested the validity of a universal international law, applicable not only among the Christian nations of the West but among all peoples of the world, on the principle of sociability—that "human nature itself," in his words, "causes us to desire a mutual society."

And yet—look at us! The peoples of the world share a global ethic, yet they are still consumed by ethnic and territorial passions, by ties of blood and soil. We have authentic universal religious and humanist creeds that support a global ethic, yet we are only beginning to develop a body of world law that embodies that ethic.

Which takes me to good faith, including both justice and mercy.

GLOBAL LAW CAN EMERGE FROM FAITH

For present purposes, allow me to distinguish faith from both religion and morality, though it is closely related to both. I would emphasize in "religion" the importance of doctrines, of teachings, concerning what is sacred, what is holy, what is transcendent, what gives ultimate meaning to life. This includes, of course, moral teachings, ethics, but looks beyond them to their source and inspiration. "Faith" adds both to doctrine and to morals a commitment, not only a belief that there is a God, or that there are spiritual values transcending material self interest, but also a belief in those spiritual values, a commitment to them, an acceptance of responsibility to serve them. Faith involves feelings—feelings of dependence, gratitude, humility, obligation. It comes from the heart. It is our willingness to live out our beliefs, to sacrifice for them, even to die for them if necessary. Such faith may not be religious in the doctrinal sense; it may be faith in the nation, or faith in democracy. It has a social dimension. I follow H. Richard Niebuhr in emphasizing that faith brings human beings together in communities of trust and loyalty. "Faith," Niebuhr writes in his *Radical Monotheism and Western Culture*, "is embodied in social institutions as well as in private institutions, in corporate endeavors as well as in individual activities, in secular pursuits as well as sacred expressions."

A common spiritual faith is needed to support the emerging law of the emerging world society, a spiritual faith grounded in history but adapted to a new millennium of global integration. Such a common spiritual faith must draw, I believe, on the resources not only of Christianity, Judaism, and Islam but also of various other religions as well as on various kinds of humanism that share with religions a belief in the priority of spiritual values over material values, the priority of sociability over material self-interest. I believe that we are already entering the new age, which may come to be called the age of the holy spirit.

I speak of a common spiritual faith rather than of a common ethic or a common religion, and I speak of the kind of spiritual faith that is needed to support a legal order that crosses all ethnic, territorial, cultural, and religious boundaries.

WORLD LAW AND WORLD RELIGION

Let me give a simple example of a significant body of world law that now exists, and has existed for centuries, that is supported by the good faith of those who create it and are governed by it, namely, the so-called law merchant. I refer to the body of law that governs domestic and transnational commercial transactions—export-import contracts, contracts of carriage of goods by sea and rail and truck and air, marine insurance, payment by letters of credit issued by banks. If, for example, goods are shipped from California to New York by vessel via the Panama Canal, the ocean bill of lading will normally have the same legal character as an ocean bill of

PROPHETIC VOICES

If law continues in the service of religion and discriminates on a religious basis it will hinder the free flow of ideas and the fostering of respect, and will remain an enemy of those it marginalizes. Secularism is the panacea, as long as it is a secularism that holds neither one nor all religion over the other.

Syed Adnan Hussain
J.D./M.T.S.,
Emory University, 2007
Ph.D. Candidate,
University of Toronto

PROPHETIC VOICES

Serving God wittily means understanding law in relation to faith and appreciating that the law is only authentic law if it is true to the dignity of those persons God created in His own image.

Jean Bethke Elshtain
University of Chicago

lading used in an export-import transaction between enterprises in any two different countries of the world: It will constitute a receipt for the goods, it will contain the terms of the contract of carriage, and it will be a document of title, whose transfer to another constitutes to a transfer of ownership of goods. Likewise a domestic letter-of-credit transaction will normally be subject to the same rules that govern letter-of-credit transactions between citizens of different countries. The exporters and importers of the world, the bankers of the world, the marine insurance underwriters of the world, the long-distance carriers of the world, and others associated with them, including their lawyers, form a world community that over the centuries has made, and continues to make, through their contractual relations with each other, the law by which their various types of transactions are governed. Formally, the law applicable to such commercial transactions may be the law of a particular nation-state, but the court of the nation-state will enforce the contract terms and the body of transnational customary mercantile law that underlies them.

PROPHETIC VOICES

The future of law and religion in the world will be one in which religion continues to serve as a touchstone for law. ... Religion proffers that sheer force does not create just law ... [and] ... religion tempers the claims of even good and legitimate laws by reminding the state that individuals have more than one allegiance and authority—not only to the state and its laws, but also to their religion.

Joel A. Nichols
J.D./M.Div.,
Emory University, 2000
Associate Professor of Law,
University of St. Thomas
School of Law

What is the belief-system, the ethic, the faith that underlies and supports a universal body of mercantile law—as it is coming to underlie a growing body of world financial law, world law of investment, and other branches of the law of the world economy? The answer usually given is that it is in the "material self-interest" of merchants and banks to have a body of law governing the sale of goods. And that, of course, is true. But self-interest hardly explains it. There is also a shared ethic, a shared belief that contracts should be binding, that promises should be kept. Most important, there is also a shared faith in the community of merchants and bankers who make the trade terms and credit terms and who come together periodically in the International Chamber of Commerce in Paris to revise them, a shared trust that the people who constitute the market will not degenerate into a body of scoundrels and thieves, a shared belief in the law by which the mercantile and banking and shipping and underwriting communities are governed. I might note that the International Chamber of Commerce is a global federation of national committees of business enterprises from about 65 different countries plus individual members from approximately 110 countries. Over 50,000 enterprises are represented in it.

Another striking example is the law of sport, including especially the law governing the Olympic Games. Here a special tribunal, the International Court of Arbitration of Sport in Lausanne, Switzerland, decides cases and lays down rules governing what has become not only a multimillion-dollar world business, but also remains a passionate manifestation of world community. In addition to transnational communities of enterprises engaged in economic activities, there are many other types of transnational communities that are engaged in influencing the growth of other branches of world law: transnational associations of natural scientists and of social scientists, transnational associations of doctors and of lawyers, transnational educational associations, transnational labor associations, transnational social organizations, including so-called International Nongovernmental Organizations ("INGOs"), of which more than 6,000 are registered with the United Nations. Such multinational organizations as Amnesty International, which intervenes on behalf of victims of violation of human rights, and Greenpeace, with some 6 million members, which conducts programs to protect the world environment, have a direct effect on the enforcement—and in some instances the creation—of world law. One could go on a very long time with this list, and one could recount the changes in world humanitarian law, world environmental law, world health law, and other branches of world law that such associations have fostered.

PROPHETIC VOICES

Asking questions about everything we encounter in the world challenges comfortable convictions and can be frightening; however, we can be encouraged by centuries of human commitment to critical thought and its role in the realization of hope.

Caroline Branch
J.D./M.Div.,
Emory University, 2007
Associate, King & Spalding

COMMITMENT TO COMMON SPIRITUAL VALUES CRITICAL

I conclude by reiterating that in the historical context of an emerging and still fragile global order, a transnational, cross-cultural, inter-religious commitment to spiritual values is needed, if ethnic and territorial and other diverse cultural forces of disintegration are not to frustrate the formation of world law, a world society, and eventually a world community. I have called the new age into which mankind is entering the age of the holy spirit; this is an ecumenical age which not only corresponds to Christian tradition but is also congenial to adherents of other religions as well as to those humanists who disclaim religious affiliation but nevertheless hold spiritual values to be sacred. I believe that only a shared faith in the common destiny of mankind gradually to form a world community will provide the vision and the support necessary to the continued creation of a world order governed by law, and that a belief in world law is necessary to provide the vision and the support necessary to the establishment of a world religion.

This essay was written for the silver anniversary celebration of the Center for the Study of Law and Religion.

The great English poet T.S. Eliot once wrote that: "Religions run wild must be tamed, for they cannot be long caged." Religion is an ineradicable condition of human lives and human communities. Religion will invariably figure in our legal and political lives—however forcefully the community might seek to repress or deny its value or validity, however cogently the academy might logically bracket it from its political and legal calculus. Religion must be dealt with, because it exists—perennially, profoundly, pervasively, in every community. It must be drawn into a constructive alliance with a regime of law, democracy, and human rights.

John Witte, Jr.
God's Joust, God's Justice, 2006

IN THE END

THE POINT OF CONVERGENCE

Law. Religion. Those old—and young—aquaintances: How are they doing? In 25 years of conversation at the Center for the Study of Law and Religion at Emory University, what have they learned?

For starters, try these: Law and religion have realized that they may never see entirely eye to eye. That they actually have quite a lot in common. That, in fact, there's hope for productive negotiation. And that their conversation must go on.

In the Center's work these past two and a half decades, law and religion have dramatically converged. Jurists, theologians, activists from the corners of the earth have intersected—questioning, concurring, debating—at our conferences and public lectures. Clashing ideologies and practices have met in our wide-ranging studies and published works.

Through seven projects—whose breakthroughs still reverberate in classrooms, courtrooms, and congregations—perspectives from a range of legal systems and religious faiths have undergone intensive scrutiny. The projects' questions, however, continue to stretch and bend:

> *What do Christianity and democracy have to say to each other as political conditions shift, as religious fundamentalism terrorizes the world?*
>
> *Even if religion and human rights work together, what progress can we expect to ensure religious freedom for all, and how soon?*
>
> *How can we discern whether proselytism sows deliverance or discord?*
>
> *When we sound the cry of the marginalized, who hears? Who acts?*
>
> *Where religious and cultural tradition is knotted with political interest, how can the voice of reason prevail?*
>
> *How can either jurists or clergy satisfactorily sort out snarled issues related to sex, marriage, and family as once-reliable norms collapse?*
>
> *If keeping watch on children is a task for everyone, whose authority will hold sway?*

Convergence, then, is not the outcome, but the starting point. From this place of meeting and merging, new paths lead outward in many directions.

PROPHETIC VOICES

The Center has proved itself both pioneer and prophet. Its leaders foresaw the need for this kind of inquiry and set out to make it happen in a sustained push whose momentum has never slowed. At the 25-year milestone, the Center now looks toward other clamoring questions and urgent issues:

"My question for the future phase of the Center is how to appeal to and respond to the human in all of us globally."
Abdullahi Ahmed An-Na'im

"Terrorism is one of the most crucial examples of the importance of the interdisciplinary discussion of law and religion."
Don S. Browning

"I believe over the next several years that issues of family … will be front and center in the interplay between law and religion in the United States."
Michael J. Broyde

"The role of economic globalization is going to be important to study in the next quarter century."
Timothy P. Jackson

I believe that the patterns of human laws over time will reflect something of the meaning of religious truth, and that the patterns of religious truth over time will, in turn, reflect something of the measure of divine laws.

John Witte, Jr.
God's Joust, God's Justice

"We've got to find a way of talking … with those people who are falling outside of the establishments, outside of the religious institutions, because there's an enormous religious energy there."
Mark D. Jordan

"The tangled relationship between the sacred and the secular, the state and the church, is likely to be, and certainly ought to be, central to most of what the Center discusses and researches over the next 25 years."
Philip L. Reynolds

"Many of the mainstream religions of the world … do not believe that one has the right to change your religion or belief. … That is a problem we will have to look at much more closely."
Johan D. van der Vyver

"The Center could bring together scholars and policy-makers and put the best minds in this country, and perhaps around the world, together to … make improvements in the lives of children."
Karen L. Worthington

WHAT'S THE POINT?

The intersection of law and religion, these converging inevitables, creates an intriguing paradox.

Law, by its first definition, is "a binding practice or custom of a community." *Religion*, rooted in the Latin *re* + *ligare*, literally means to bind again, to bind back, or to bind anew. Both systems seek in some way to secure and stabilize, whether for the sake of a smooth-running society or the sake of relationship with the divine. As CSLR Senior Fellow and our "Chief" Harold J. Berman wrote in his 2007 essay "Law and Religion in the Age of the Holy Spirit" (see page 93), the two systems together also have the stunning potential to unite the world's people in a global society of understanding and trust.

Paradoxically, to accomplish this unity among peoples, law and religion must establish certain binding practices and customs, and they must bind, or re-bind, hearts to a shared sense of spirituality based on common principles rather than on common doctrine. They must not, however, bind each other—for in that binding, the hard-won freedom of unity can quickly dissolve.

In light of this paradoxical convergence, this working together that so easily can become working at odds, an important question remains: *What's the point of such a convergence? Ultimately, what justifies the Center's existence?*

In his essay, Harold Berman offers an answer and a transcendent ideal: "It is the lawyer's responsibility, and the lawyer's opportunity to help to construct a world order that is founded on justice, mercy, and good faith."

SUPPORTERS OF THE CENTER FOR THE STUDY OF LAW AND RELIGION

We give thanks for the generous contributions to the Center for the Study of Law and Religion from the following institutions and individuals:

MAJOR EMORY CONTRIBUTORS

Emory College

Office of the Provost

School of Law

School of Theology

MAJOR OUTSIDE CONTRIBUTORS

Alonzo L. McDonald Family Foundation

The Ford Foundation

Lilly Endowment Inc.

Henry Luce Foundation, Inc.

John Templeton Foundation

The Pew Charitable Trusts, Inc.

OTHER CONTRIBUTORS

The James Luther Adams Foundation, Inc.

Professor and Mrs. Frank S. Alexander

The Andreas Foundation

Mr. Andy and Mrs. Michelle Barclay

BellSouth Matching Gifts Program

Mrs. Jean Robitscher Bergmark

Mr. John Brabner-Smith, Esq.

Mr. and Mrs. Paul Cadenhead, Esq.

Overton and Lavonna Currie Foundation

Mr. Herman Dooyeweerd, Jr.

Fannie Mae Foundation

Fieldstead & Company

Georgia Bar Foundation

Ms. Ronit Hoffer

Mr. Case Hoogendoorn, Esq.

Hoogendoorn, Miller, Talbot and Davids

Mr. & Mrs. W. Stell Huie

Dean and Mrs. Howard O. Hunter

Mr. Erich Kennedy, Esq.

Dr. Marion Leathers Kuntz

Liberty Fund

Mr. Lansing B. Lee, Esq.

Local Initiatives Support Corporation (L.I.S.C.)

The Joe and Emily Lowe Foundation, Inc.

Mr. Russell B. Mabrey, Esq.

Mr. John Mayoue, Esq.

Professor Charlotte McDaniel

Mr. Albert G. Moore

Mr. Terrill A. Parker, Esq.

Mr. Stuart D. Poppel, Esq.

Mr. Kenneth W. Ramsey, Esq.

The Reebok Foundation

Mr. George R. Salem, Esq.

The Steinhardt Foundation – EDAH

The Bernard Stern Foundation, Inc.

Alexander von Humboldt Stiftung

Mr. and Mrs. Randolph W. Thrower

United Church Board for Homeland Ministries

Dr. and Mrs. Magnus Verbrugge

Professor John Witte, Jr. and Ms. Eliza Ellison

ABOUT THE AUTHORS

April L. Bogle is Director of Public Relations and Information for the Center for the Study of Law and Religion at Emory University. She produces award-winning communication programs for corporations and non-profit organizations.

Ginger Pyron, Ph.D. (Vanderbilt University), with long experience in values-based marketing and consulting for academic institutions, is a writer and creative consultant based in Atlanta.

ACKNOWLEDGMENTS

COPYEDITING

Eliza Ellison
Lynn Klein
Amy Wheeler
John Witte, Jr.

PHOTOGRAPHY

Flip Chalfant
Dan Dry
Corky Gallo
Carolyn Wright
Emory University Photo Department

GRAPHIC DESIGN

Jim and Hollis Wise, WisenKlein Communications

ILLUSTRATION

James Turner

PROJECT COORDINATION

Tasha Schroeder

PRINTING

Prographics Communications, Inc.